'You Must E[illegible]

The story of a Himalayan 'Trek of Hope'

MICHAEL JAMES

Publish & Print
www.publishandprint.co.uk

Published July 2020
ISBN: 9798663447126

3 Beatty Avenue
Roath Park
Cardiff
CF23 5QR

The Just Giving page for donations to the two charities, The Leprosy Mission, England and Wales and Rainbow of Hope is:
www.justgiving.com/wltlm

Websites:
www.leprosymission.org.uk
www.facebook.com/RainbowofHopeCardiff
https://fatmantunepal.blogspot.com

‘In memory of four friends, Paul Jenkins and Peter Lewis, who taught me that difficulties are there to be overcome and Ken Bowen and Philip Begley who encouraged me to share my story.'

Published by
www.publishandprint.co.uk

Acknowledgments

My grateful thanks go to:

John West who first encouraged me to expand my journal into a book.

Beryl Jones for her expertise and invaluable help in the format of the book and correction of grammar and spelling mistakes.

Roger and Mary Leadbeter and William (Bill) Oliver for their proof reading and constant support.

Sue and Roger Irwin and many, many others, for their prayers which helped me enormously and without which I would not have been able to carry on.

Dawa Geljen Sherpa and his team from Adventure Themserku (Nepal).

Dave Lewis (Publish & Print - www.publishandprint.co.uk) for his patient understanding and helpful advice, without which this book would not have become a reality.

Dawa and Bill for writing their commendations for this book, based on their understanding and knowledge of how difficult a challenge the trek was for me.

My trekking companions; Grace, Dani, Shelia, John, Hugh, Chris, Andy, the two Steve's, Sarah and Jeff, for kindly allowing me to use their photographs in this book.

My children, Gareth and Caroline, Derian and Richard and my grandchildren, Holly, Maisy, Seren and Louis, for all their help in getting Granddad's great adventure known through the world of modern information technology.

Lastly (certainly, not least) and much more importantly, my wife, Elizabeth, who, initially did not want me to undertake such a venture, but became my greatest supporter and encourager of my 'Trek of Hope'.

'Elizabeth, I could not have done any of this without your love and understanding'.

Commendation

Michael and I and our respective families have been friends for many years which makes it a great privilege and pleasure to write this foreword to his book which is a story of several trips he has made to Nepal and India because of his love and commitment to the work of The Leprosy Mission. His visits to several leprosy hospitals and colonies and his love and compassion for those suffering from the disease is very apparent in his book, as well as his work for the Rainbow of Hope helping the homeless and disadvantaged in Cardiff.

For many years, Michael has been our Church's Representative for TLM but it has been in recent years that he has taken his level of commitment to new heights and which led him to undertake his personal, 'Trek of Hope', in the Himalayas, which is the centre piece of the book. It starts with his dilemma as to whether this venture was his own desire or a call from God, which he refers to as a 'niggling, still, small voice'. When all the different obstacles kept cropping up, (the trip was off and then back on), they seemed to heighten God's call and his own desire, equally and, I suppose that it was inevitable to be a mixture of both.

I accompanied Michael on two walks for TLM in the Brecon Beacons and on both occasions I was a 'back marker' to keep an
eye on him. We had to take many rests before finishing a long time after the other walkers, with him in a state of near collapse.

When I heard that he was considering trekking in the Himalayas, I don't know if I actually voiced it at the time or whether I just thought "you must be crazy". All I do know is that, completing his 'Trek of Hope', was nothing short of a miracle.

On reading the book one becomes aware of the very strong emphasis on prayer and also of his faith, which enabled him to get over the line. There is also much on the wonderful healing ministries of both The Leprosy Mission and the Rainbow of Hope among the people they serve in God's name and for His Glory. This truly is a book to inspire and encourage.

William Oliver
Friend and Church Elder

Commendation

It gives me great pleasure to write this foreword to Michael's book, as it shows that first impressions are not always what they seem. Over the years I have led many trekking expeditions in the Himalayas of Nepal, Tibet, India and Bhutan and met hundreds of different people from all walks of life and of all nationalities.

Michael is no different to the many before him and since, who have come excitedly and expectantly for the trek that lay ahead of them but my first impression on meeting him was that he looked overweight and unfit and I wondered if he would be able to make it. I was not far wrong, but, what I couldn't see was the inner core of determination and commitment that would see him rise to the challenge. There are people who fear the challenge and give up before the experience and others who undertake the challenge and are determined to see what is waiting on the other side. Michael is the second kind of person.

Each day he struggled to cope with the heat, the altitude and the physicality of the climb but never once did he complain, always had a smile on his face and his only worry was that he was concerned about falling behind his trekking companions and delaying them.

They, in turn, were concerned about him and each evening welcomed him 'home', with encouraging applause. His sheer determination to get to the end of each day's climb and his unfailing good humour endeared him to his companions. For many in the group he was their motivation, they moved on a step more because they knew he was following them. Each of them had struggled in their own way so that they realised just how great an effort it was for him. He will say he had help, not only from their encouragement and that of the professional Guides and Sherpas but also from his God who, he says, was with him 'every step of the way' and in Whose strength, enabled him to complete the challenge to the benefit of his two charities.

A remarkable man in many ways and someone I am proud to call my friend.

Dawa Geljen Sherpa
Trek Leader. Adventure Themserku

Contents

Introduction

I have been encouraged to write this book by those who have heard my story and felt that it should be shared. I write about my Trek in the Himalayas for the same reasons as I undertook the trek, which was to raise awareness of Leprosy and Homelessness and raise funding for the ongoing work of the two charities I work with as a volunteer, The Leprosy Mission, England and Wales and Rainbow of Hope (Paradise Run).

In many ways both these Charities have the same Christian ethos. They work to provide help and hope by serving those in need; the outcasts; those shunned by society; cast aside by all, even members of their own families. The unclean; the unwanted; those with no homes and nowhere to sleep safely at night; no clean or dry clothing; no food; no warmth and with little or no chance of employment.

They feel worthless, with no hope and no love, except from these two Charities I work with and it is the that I undertook the difficult (for me) challenge of my 'Trek of Hope'.

This book is written from a personal perspective in my Christian belief that it was what God wanted me to do and He equipped me to fulfil that task but I fully understand and respect that some may believe in another god or deity or perhaps not have any faith.

Nevertheless, I hope that in reading it someone might

be given the hope and encouragement that they (yourself perhaps?) who believe that they may be too old or unable to get up and do something (not necessarily climbing mountains) which can benefit others and in doing so gain benefits themselves by climbing and overcoming their personal mountains of the difficulties they face daily. I sincerely hope that it will.

To quote my late dear friend Paul Jenkins, "Don't just think about it, go out and do it!".

The Leprosy Mission (TLM)

TLM is an international Christian organisation that diagnoses, treats and offers specialist care, including reconstructive surgery, to those suffering from leprosy. It also provides rehabilitation, education and vocational training to tens of thousands of people to provide a springboard to restored health, self-sufficiency and renewed hope. These services are provided regardless of religion or ethnicity, promoting equality and social justice to those suffering with leprosy.

When I mention the work of TLM to people, their reaction is generally, "Is leprosy still about?", or, "Isn't that a historical/biblical disease?".

Well yes it is still about and no, it is not historical but very much of today. Although curable if detected in its early stages, leprosy is a crippling, disfiguring, blinding disease which effects approximately three million people worldwide, especially across, Asia, Africa and

Brazil. Figures published by the World Health Organisation show that around a quarter of a million cases are diagnosed globally each year and at least six people will have been diagnosed as having Leprosy by the time you have finished reading this foreword. TLM, although receiving some funding from governments, also relies heavily on donations from the general public.

The Leprosy Mission, England, and Wales
Goldhay Way,
Orton Goldhay,
Peterborough. PE2 5GZ.
Registered Charity Number 1050327.
Telephone 01733 370505.
e-mail: post@tlmew.org.uk

Rainbow of Hope (Paradise Run)

This is a small, local organisation which works among the homeless and disadvantaged in Cardiff. Started twenty two years ago by a lady, Elizabeth Perret-Atkins, who felt called by God to go out, on her own, each night on the streets of Wales' capital city to feed those in need.

Upon learning about her work, others joined her and now the charity, run by a small group of unpaid staff, operates a small office cum shop, cafe and drop-in advice centre. Voluntary helpers from other local churches in Cardiff and the South Wales Valleys, go out onto the City's streets every single night of the year providing hot food, sandwiches, hot drinks, sleeping bags and clothing. It also provides food parcels to many in need, single parents, refugees and asylum seekers in the local community. It receives no funding from official bodies and exists solely on donations, mostly food and clothing, from the generosity of the public.

Since the opening of the shop, with it's bible study and prayer groups five people have given themselves to God and have turned their lives around.

Rainbow of Hope
23-25 Broadway,
Cardiff. CF24 1QE
Registered Charity Number, 1088856.
Telephone 029 2049 4317.
e-mail: info@rainbowofhope.co.uk

Part 1
WHY?

1
A Still, Small Voice

'You must be Crazy!', or something very similar, was the response I received when I told family, friends and my church fellowship that I was thinking of undertaking a sponsored Trek in the Himalayas.

I have to say that there is the basis of truth in their initial reaction because, let's face it, it would be a serious challenge for anyone, especially me. I am not the enthusiastic, athletic, Bear Grylls type of person. Bear is a former British SAS, all action hero who scaled Everest at the tender age of 23 and I was, at the time I decided to undertake the Trek, an unfit, overweight, 75 year old, with arthritic knees, high blood pressure, suffering with a mild form of epilepsy, type 2 diabetes and possibly, a mild form of old age crisis. Yes, people's general reaction was probably sensible and deep down I too wondered if I should do it.

Then why? Quite simply, for many years I have felt God calling me to do something for Him. To serve others in some way or another and His 'still small voice' had been in my head every day. My biggest concerns were twofold. Was it something that I should or could do and was it really God challenging me or, was it just some fanciful idea of my own?

Some twenty years ago, I read that The Leprosy Mission (TLM), was inviting some of its supporters to go on a sponsored bicycle ride through India to raise funds and awareness for its work among those suffering from leprosy.

This was it, I thought, even though at the time I didn't own a bike and had not ridden one for some thirty odd years.

Still you never forget how to ride and I could always buy a bike.

I wrote to TLM to apply for a place on the bike ride and while awaiting a reply I found an old, unwanted, racing bike at the local Council refuse tip. "Yes you can have it", the man said. To me this was the confirmation I needed. I was on my way to India.

The old bike needed some urgent, tender loving care, so I took it to a local bicycle repair shop for a thorough overhaul. Two weeks later, I went to collect it. Now sporting new tyres, new brakes and overhauled gears, it was ready to go but was I?

Outside the shop, I confidently mounted my iron steed and set off. Not the most elegant of starts, wobbling and swaying from side to side I took nearly two hours to travel the three miles to my home. My wife, Elizabeth, following me in the car had to stop driving on one occasion, overcome with a mixture of laughter and concern at my progress but she and I eventually arrived home safely.

For the next month or so I went out riding every day, usually in the early evening when the traffic was not too heavy. I became more proficient in going in a straight line and my rides were getting longer. However, I was getting more and more nervous on the main roads and the thought of the much heavier, chaotic traffic and unsurfaced roads and tracks in India gave me much cause for concern.

I spoke to Elizabeth and we prayed about the

situation and reluctantly came to the sensible conclusion that I shouldn't go. Dejected and somewhat downhearted, I informed TLM that I was withdrawing my application. My dream was over. Perhaps it would be better to stick with helping support the work of my two Charities by giving them the cost of the trip instead.

2
A Taste of India

Time moved on and the months and years passed but never a day went by when the thought of that missed opportunity was out of mind. I should have had faith. I should have just got on with it. If God had wanted me to do it, surely, somehow, He would have let me know. Perhaps it just wasn't meant to happen. Perhaps, after all, it really was just my own little fantasy.

Then, out of the blue TLM announced that there would be no more bike rides but it was considering doing a sponsored trek in the Himalayas instead. This was the moment I had been waiting for, something that was in the realms of possibility, I was good at walking and apart from having to buy a pair of sturdy boots I thought that's really all there was to it.

Excitedly, I mentioned it to my wife, Elizabeth, who, ever the sensible one, said, "Really! Do you think that you are up to such a challenge?" This was probably the original version of, "You must be crazy!" She didn't actually say, "I don't want you to go," but it was quite obvious that was her position. So I went away to reconsider the idea and the more I thought about it, I came to the conclusion that she was right.

Despite my believing that this was what God was leading me to do, logic took over from faith and all the practicalities of such a venture started to prove to be too difficult for someone of my advanced age and condition. It really didn't seem sensible and I backed that up by telling myself that I could never ask people to sponsor me or donate to something I could and perhaps would, easily fail to do.

Reluctantly, once again, I decided not to proceed. Instead I went on a Supporters trip to India in 2010, to see at first hand TLM's work among those suffering from leprosy.

So it was that on the 15 March 2010, I travelled with Jean, another TLM supporter from Wales, to meet the rest of our fellow travellers at Heathrow airport. Including Jean and I, our party of twenty was made up from of sixteen other TLM supporters from other parts of England, plus two staff from the Mission's headquarters at Peterborough.

On our arrival at Delhi airport, we were driven to the YWCA which was to be our base while in Delhi.

It was not a hotel as I had expected but a hostel, perfectly adequate for our purposes. Centrally located to enable us to walk to the bustling centre of the City which was in the process of a lot of construction work, updating the road structure in preparation of the upcoming Commonwealth Games later that year. What was disturbing to us, however was the number of homeless people, men, women and children, sleeping or begging or playing in amongst the dust and filth of the road works, while all the time, the chaos of the busy traffic went on around them as did the cows and other animals that were everywhere. Welcome to India!

We were taken to The Leprosy Mission hospital at Shahdara, Delhi, where we we given an introduction to all the medical work that was going on there and at the other hospitals we were going to visit during our stay. Shahdara covers around two million people in the area surrounding the hospital. It has a staff of thirty, surgeons, doctors, nurses, health workers, pharmacy and physiotherapy staff. It has forty five in-bed patient beds and also runs out-patient clinics. The standard of both eye and limb surgery and all the other general medical work is so good that local hospitals send their own staff to observe and train alongside the TLM teams. Shahdara hospital has now become part of the Indian Government General Heath Care System but is funded directly by TLM India.

We then travelled to see the 'Village of Hope', one of five leprosy colonies in East Delhi where we spent a pleasant afternoon with some of the 5,000 people who lived there, celebrating the Women's World Day of Prayer with a lovely meal, then back to our hotel before supper and bed. An early breakfast and then a four hour drive to Agra and a visit to the beautiful Taj Mahal (See more later).

3
'A Challenge'

The next morning we arrived at the main railway station to make the six hour journey to Lucknow. We had reserved seats but they were scattered throughout the compartment and I was seated alongside an Indian family. We exchanged pleasantries about the early start, crowded trains etc. and then the father said to me, "There seems to be a lot of Europeans travelling today. Are you all together and where are you going?" My heart nearly stopped and I struggled to answer. I was aware of the huge stigma leprosy has in India and had read stories of people being hounded off public transport because of the association with the disease. I didn't want to risk the possibility of that happening however unlikely, so I simply replied, "Yes, we are travelling around India visiting hospitals to see if we can offer any help". This seemed to satisfy him but I was consumed with guilt. It was as if, like Peter denying three times before the cock crowed, that he wasn't one of the group that knew Jesus, I had been challenged and been found wanting but even with that in my mind I still couldn't find myself able to tell the man the truth for fear of being caught out in my lie. I just sat there for a while and pretended to sleep but in reality I was deep in prayer asking God to forgive my weakness and to strengthen my resolve. After a few miles the train came to a stop and the man and his family left, leaving me rueing the chance to witness. Another few miles and we came to another station and a business man came to sit alongside me. Once again after a few polite words our conversation turned to the question of our presence on the train.

This time I faced the question head on and without hesitation answered, "We are supporters of a Christian organisation, The Leprosy Mission, and are visiting the leprosy hospitals and colonies to see the work going on among those suffering and to raise funding for them". The man took this answer at face value and asked many questions about leprosy that I was more than happy to answer. God really does provide us with opportunities to witness and equips us to do His work.

Arriving at Lucknow we boarded a bus for a drive to Faizabad where, after spending a welcome, restful day followed by a leisurely meal, we took the opportunity of an early night. The next morning we attended the daily Church Service, at TLM's Vocational Training Centre together with the VTC students, young men and women, some of whom have leprosy and others who live with their leprosy affected parents. They spend up to two years studying to gain a nationally recognised degree or diploma with which they can find suitable employment, which in turn, as well as much needed income for themselves and their families, brings them the great added benefit of self esteem.

At the other end of the scale, 'so to speak', Faizabad has a TLM Snehalaya (Mercy Home), which provides long stay accommodation for many elderly patients who would otherwise be homeless having been abandoned by their families because they had leprosy. An overnight stay at Faizabad, then the next morning a bus ride to Lucknow to catch our train back to Delhi where we visited a leprosy colony at Faridabad and

TLM hospitals in Delhi, Bankura and Barabanki where I gained a really good insight into the surgical and medical work.

At the end of our visit to see the work of TLM, the main party flew home and I stayed on as I had arranged to see Kolkata (Calcutta) and Mumbai (Bombay), as I had thought that it would probably my first and only trip to India. To get from Delhi to Kolkata involved a 17-hour, overnight sleeper train ride during which I was to share a two berth compartment with an Indian businessman. We got on very well together and full of new found confidence I quite easily told him why I was there and he wanted to know all about my two charities.

Kolkata is a wonderfully diverse city full of noise, colour and seemingly, with almost as many different forms of vehicles as people, all bringing the streets to a standstill and with car, bus and lorry horns all adding to the cacophony of sound. I had arranged a tour of the city and was taken to many of the historical and cultural sites, one of which was, 'The Mother House' where Mother Teresa cared for the poor and sick, including the dozens of orphans, many with debilitating illnesses who were being cared for by many Christian and other Faiths volunteers from all over the world.

4
Obstacles

My time in India was a wonderful experience, both inspiring and humbling at the same time. I returned home reasonably satisfied that I had got the idea of trekking out of my mind.

This was further helped by going on a nine mile sponsored walk in the Brecon Beacons with my friend Bill Oliver, during which I found myself practically climbing up the steep mountains on all fours. If I couldn't handle this, what chance of trekking in the Himalayas?

Despite this humbling experience, it did some good by raising funds for the work of TLM, so the next year, 2011, I decided to try the walk in the Beacons again. This time, with the extra help of two stout walking poles I fared much better but even so I still finished last of the group some way behind the others. I was convinced that my trekking days were over but little did I know......!

For the next few months the challenge of a trek was in my head every day, invading almost all my waking hours, so much so that I once again mentioned it to Elizabeth who simply said, "OK, if that is what you want to do, then do it."

Needing no second thoughts I looked on-line and to my delight found that TLM was arranging another trek in 2012. Excitedly I asked for my name to be put on the list and set about finding out what I needed to do to prepare me for the adventure that lay ahead.

Then in July I received a telephone call to tell

me that the trek had been cancelled due to lack of participants making it financially non viable but the voice said, perhaps hoping to lessen the blow, "TLM Scotland is planning a similar trek in October 2012." I quickly rang Scotland, only to be told that the last places had been filled that very week. Once again my hopes had been dashed but still believing that this was what God wanted me to do, I again prayed that something would work out for me.

Several weeks later I read that TLM Australia was considering making a trek in Nepal. I needed no second bidding to get in touch with the Australian office by e-mail and was informed that I could join them but their Trek would not take place until November 2014. "Too far off I thought", as it was now December 2012 and I was getting older. So I rang TLM England and Wales to ask for the name of the Trekking Company which had arranged their previous treks. This company said they would try to find me a place on someone else's trek. By the following February I had heard nothing so I decided to explore what other trekking companies had to offer. One had a trek in April that year. Too soon! Another in the October 2013.

This was a possibility, so they pencilled in my name. A little later, one of my arthritic knees started giving me problems and I ended up hobbling around for two months. On top of that the trekking company rang to say that because of lack of interest, their October trek was cancelled but they would definitely have one in April 2014 if I was interested. "Good I thought", this would give me more time for my knee to heal, so I provisionally signed up.

When I shared these continuing problems, one

of my closest friends said, "Perhaps it is God telling you it's not what He wants you to do!" I don't know where my reply came from but I confidently replied, "It's not God that's putting obstacles in my way, it's 'the other guy. If God wants me to do it, He will help me overcome all my difficulties."

Despite this outward show of confidence, there was little more that I could do except pray. On the plus side my knee was getting better and the small voice in my head kept speaking to me, so much so that I spoke with a good friend of mine, an Anglican priest about it. "How," I wanted to know, "Can I decide if it is God's voice or mine?" His reply was, "When you simply cannot get it out of your mind, it's God speaking to you."

That gave me the encouragement I needed and when I told Elizabeth, she said, "OK, then that's what you must do. Go for it!" This brought to mind the attitude of two friends of mine, sadly no longer with us. Paul Jenkins, although blind. was an athlete who had run a hundred marathons and had even raced up the stairs of New York's Empire State Building. On two occasions! His mantra was simple. "Don't just think about doing things, go ahead and do them!" Also there was Peter Lewis, who had severe physical disabilities and had lost one eye from infection, always said that, "Disability is not inability! God will provide you with what you need."

Their approach to life and their trust in God, was and still is, truly inspiring.

5
Confirmation

That same evening, Elizabeth and I attended the weekly prayer meeting in church and the leader read from the book of Joshua, chapter 14, verse 11, where Caleb, at the great age of 85, said, "Give me the hill country that the Lord promised me," confident that whatever the difficulties which lay ahead, God would see him through them all, not in Caleb's own strength but in God's strength. I heard this text as, "Give me a mountain." It was at that moment as if a light bulb switched on in my head and I saw clearly for the first time, what had been, up until that moment, a cloud of uncertainty. It was as if God was confirming that it was what He wanted me to do, in His Name. I shared that moment with the meeting and wave upon wave of positive prayer swept over me.

I was now certain that I should go ahead with my plans and the following day I confirmed my place on the trek starting in April 2014. I pressed on with all the practicalities and only the thought of raising enough sponsorship or donations worried me. I would be personally paying all the costs of the Trek, including airfares and hotels and I had pledged to try to raise £1,500 for each of my two charities but how and where to start? I knew that I could count on the support of family and close friends but that might not be enough. Who else could I approach? At that stage, I began to see the size of the challenge ahead of me, even before I faced the physical challenge of the Trek itself and I began to lose heart.

Then I had an idea. I could canvas support by

asking for sponsorship from the St. David's Praise Choir, some two hundred voices from local churches in South Wales, of which I was a part. I thought that the night of the first rehearsal for our Christmas concert would be the ideal place to ask but even then I was too afraid to ask for a show of hands in support and perhaps get only one or two in response. So I decided to get our Choirmaster to ask for me. To my great shame, I even made sure that I was not present at the time.

Such lack of faith didn't deserve success but I was later informed that there was overwhelming support for me.

Buoyed up by this support, the day before my 75th birthday in December 2013, I announced in Church that I was definitely going trekking in support of the work of The Leprosy Mission and the Rainbow of Hope and my training would start the very next day. Once again there were concerns from many quarters but also offers of support, both financial and, more importantly, prayer.

At this point the Trekking Company had advised all those taking part to do a minimum of fourteen weeks training, as the trek would be no sightseeing holiday but a serious challenge. Trekking for seven days, for between six to eight hours per day, at altitudes of up to 3,500 metres and sleeping in tents at night would be difficult for anyone, especially me.

I started my training early the next day, my birthday, in pouring rain which continued each day for the next week and which, coincidentally or not, found me with a very heavy cold. It was not sensible to continue in the circumstances so I decided to enjoy Christmas and put off any walking until the New Year.

Over that Christmas period, in talking things through with my family, my children came up with the brilliant idea of fund raising though social media pages, something I would not have thought about or even known where to begin They quickly set up a blog, web site and a financial giving page. They thought that it would be both funny and eye catching to call it, 'FatmantuNepal', an obvious play of words on my size and my Trek. That's children for you, no respect!

However, the fundraising couldn't go 'live' until I had sorted out the possibility of people being able to Gift Aid their donations. This was not as easy as it sounds. First I had to receive formal approval from the two charities to use their names and charity numbers and to get the appropriate gift envelopes and donation and sponsorship forms printed.

This took about a month to set up and in the meantime all I could do was to go out walking every day.

6
Physical Obstacles

Walking every day seemed to be easy enough but in reality it was a bit of a nightmare as it was done during January, February and March 2014, possibly the three wettest and wildest months on record. I had been given a 14-week training programme to bring me up to a certain level of fitness so that I could manage the rigours of the trek.

Starting on the 1st January 2014 gave me just fifteen weeks before flying out so I could not afford to miss a day, even allowing for the rest days scheduled in the programme. I started walking around a lake near my home which took me just over an hour, building this up to walks of two, three and four hours with increasing levels of steepness of climb. To make these walks more challenging, I would push my two year old grandson in his buggy, which was a bit of an effort, on the local hills around my home.

The longer four hour days were spent in the seaside town of Porthcawl, walking along its wild and windy coastal path.

Lovely scenery and very refreshing but in those weather conditions quite an effort for me but no doubt, for the greater good, I hoped! At this stage most of my walks had been on relatively flat areas or smaller hills, so now I decided to push myself harder.

Close to my home stands Caerphilly Mountain, standing at 271 metres (890 feet) above sea level, with two different roads to its summit, one quite steep and the other steeper still. For my first attempt, I chose the easier of the two routes, which took some effort but for which I rewarded myself with a nice cup of coffee at the little cafe at the top of the mountain. Suitably rested, refreshed and feeling rather pleased with myself, I set off down the mountain by the steeper route. Half way down I realised that I had made a huge mistake. My knees and shins began to ache and progress was like walking through treacle and each of the numerous stops made starting off again a great effort. When I eventually reached the bottom I made a vow that, on returning, I would climb the steepest route first and this I did on numerous subsequent occasions.

On top of Caerphilly mountain

However, getting to the top of the mountain in itself was not enough, I was beginning to do the round trip quicker each time and it was shorter than my four hour per day programme requirements. I then decided to extend the walk down from the top of the mountain into the town of Caerphilly.

This would give me the necessary longer hours and also the extra physical effort of the ascent and descent to Caerphilly and the reverse ascent and descent on my return to Cardiff, a round trip of a difficult eight miles.

I did this on a number of occasions but then had to push myself further with longer, tougher walks or climbs in the famous Brecon Beacons National Park, a rugged mountainous area which is the training ground of the British Army's Special Services and a popular trekking area.

I returned to the scene of my earlier failures of the walks with TLM in the previous two years. These poor attempts had made me think that I could never undertake trekking in the Himalayas but surely, after all my training, I thought this time it would be different.

I drove to the Beacons and confidently set off, equipped with my two walking poles to support me and make the climbing easier, which it did. My only problem this time was that I got lost. Of course I had a map with me but to my professional shame, I am a Chartered Surveyor after all, I still got lost. The first part of the route I remembered quite well but I obviously took a wrong turn somewhere and this made my eventual return to where I had left my car, even longer. I could only console myself in thinking that God was helping me to achieve a greater level of fitness by providing me with this longer 'stroll'.

The only problem was that after another few walks to Caerphilly and back, I attempted the same walk in the Beacons again and once again got lost, this time by a bigger margin. I had the huge embarrassment of having to call at a local farmhouse to ask for directions and was given a lift for a couple of miles to be put back on track, by which time it was just beginning to get dark, although I did get back to the car safely.

Summit of Pen-y-Fan

The whole experience was quite a sobering one during which I prayed a lot. I was really lost, in difficult terrain with darkness falling and no mobile phone signal. Was it my own stupidity or the work of 'the other guy'. Whichever it was, God once again heard my cries of help and got me through it. I was now more than ever convinced that He was blessing my plans.

I had another few days on shorter walks and then the big test I had set myself, to climb to the top of Pen y Fan, at 886 metres (2,906 feet), the highest point in the Brecon Beacons and indeed the whole of South Wales.

It was a perfect day for climbing, sunny but not too hot and with a gentle breeze. I chose the most difficult route to the top, straight up and however much my fitness had improved, it was a very difficult climb for me. Other younger walkers were very encouraging as they hurried past me on my numerous rest stops and were pleased to see me when I eventually reached the summit.

After an hour or so at the top, fortified by sandwiches, coffee and a good rest I set off back down the mountain, this time by a relatively easier route. I was elated, I had achieved something that I had set out to do some fourteen weeks earlier and with just another few days of gentle walks, I was ready to go.

Yes, I was ready to go, physically at least but there were yet more obstacles that seemed to be blocking my path.

7
Different Obstacles

These new obstacles were not physical but practical, logistical ones. The Trekking Company that I had signed up with came back to me earlier in the New Year to say that there was a problem with the airline. I could fly out and return with the main party but it couldn't, or wouldn't, let me fly out earlier and return later as I wanted to do. I had requested this to enable me to fly to Nepal to visit The Leprosy Mission hospital at Anandaban so that I could witness the work of TLM first hand, whilst at the same time, becoming acclimatised to the higher altitudes and, at the end of the Trek, spend a couple more days relaxing at a mountain retreat in Pokhara before returning home.

The only way around this was for me to arrange my own flights. So I got a travel agent to provisionally book the appropriate flights for me while I confirmed with my insurance company that I was covered to trek. I already had an annual policy which covered trekking but I thought it wise to check. They said that I could be covered, subject to an extra payment of £60. as I was trekking above 2,500 metres (8,200 feet). I was told that I also needed to fill in a medical questionnaire and have it signed by my doctor. This should have been no problem but, I was told, if I had any other problems over and above my stated pre-existing health problems, I would have to pay a further additional premium of £300. I prayed that there were to be none!

There was now a wait now over the weekend until I receive the signed questionnaire from my doctor but in the meantime, yet another problem arose. Due to the delay in confirming I could go, the airfare had jumped up almost £200. which, together with the possible excess insurance money, would increase my costs by another £600.

Something someone had said to me earlier came to mind, "Why not just give all the costs, approximately £2,000, directly to your two Charities, put your feet up and bask in the self praise of helping in that way?". That could have worked by providing financial support but it would not meet the second objective, that of raising awareness of the great work of the Charities and those who were struggling with the affects of leprosy and homelessness which I felt was what God wanted me to do.

I decided to go on-line to see if I could find flights that would meet my needs and was delighted to find that I could fly with Etihad Airways, at a cost that was actually slightly lower than the original price my travel agent had found me.

At last things seemed to be improving. As soon as I received the signed medical questionnaire on the Monday and cleared everything with the insurance company, I booked my flights. That same day, I rang TLM to confirm my stay at Anandaban. I also rang the Hotel Tibet International in Kathmandu to confirm my two nights stay at the start and end of the Trek period and also confirmed with the Raniban Retreat at Pokhara, my two nights stay at their mountaintop hotel.

8
On My Way

With all the difficulties now behind me I could relax and spend some time with my family but I still had a busy weekend before I set off on Easter Monday.

First, I attended the Maundy Thursday Service in church. Then on Good Friday we travelled to our family home in the Rhondda Valley to see Elizabeth's brother and sister and to exchange Easter eggs for our various grandchildren. We then went to listen to the world famous Treorchy Male Choir in concert with the Parc and Dare Brass Band and didn't arrive home until midnight. The next morning, Easter Saturday, I was up early to have a haircut and mow the front and back lawns before attending the afternoon rehearsal for the St. David's Praise Choir's concert, 'The Glory of Easter', that evening. It was a wonderful evening of musical praise but another late night, midnight again.

We were in church on Easter Sunday with the family, all ten of us, including our son and his family who had travelled from Wigan to spend the weekend with us and see me off on my big adventure. As well as being an Easter Service it was also the baptism of our friend Sam. A truly meaningful service and it was good to have the church full with many of the fellowship having their families home for Easter. It was a very full weekend which somehow managed to keep me from worrying as to what lay ahead of me.

Easter Monday, 21 April 2014. At last the day of my big adventure has come! I was so excited, I was up at 7.15am. After breakfast, I busied myself with the final sorting out of my backpack and checking passport, travel documents etc. I checked that our cars had petrol, oil and water and pumped up the tyres so that Elizabeth will not have to worry about those things while I am away. Then, shower and dress, followed by team photographs with all the family before setting off to catch the bus to Heathrow.

A family send off

I arrived at Heathrow at 4.20pm. There was then a five hour wait for my flight, scheduled for 9.20pm. At check-in, I cheekily asked if I could be upgraded, "Yes of course sir," came the reply, "That will be £500 please!", an offer which I politely declined. Into security and yet another possible problem. I was pulled aside going though the X-ray machine, something had triggered it off. After a body search which found nothing it was decided that it was probably my walking boots which had metal tie fasteners. I was wearing the boots rather than stowing them in my hold luggage, so as not to increase it's weight and so that I wouldn't lose them as they were probably the most essential part of my equipment.

Now ‘air side’ and with a two and a half hour wait before boarding. To pass the time I had a leisurely meal and contented myself sending and receiving texts on my new mobile phone which was working splendidly except that I received three voice mails which I couldn’t open. In the middle of sending a text to one of the missed calls, one of my friends rang again and I was able to have a chat with him. I made a final call to Elizabeth to say that I couldn’t open my voice mail and from now on, except in an emergency, we would have to communicate only by text.

I finally, boarded my Etihad flight which left on time and was pleased that I had been allocated a window seat with plenty of leg room. After about a hour reading my newspaper, dinner was served which was very nice. I then settled down to try to get some sleep but couldn’t, which was not unusual as I can rarely sleep whilst flying and then spent the next few hours watching films before having breakfast at about 6.00am and landing at Abu Dhabi at 7.15am. There then followed almost an hour’s walk inside the building to Terminal 1 and my flight to Kathmandu. As befitted a major international hub, Abu Dhabi airport was crammed with people with long, long queues at check-in desks for flights to all parts of the world. It’s not a thing many of us usually consider but the movement of millions of people on a daily basis is staggering in its scale.

Fortunately for me the number of people waiting for my flight to Kathmandu was considerably smaller and in no time at all I was comfortably seated, once again in a window seat, eating an early lunch, for the five hour journey to Nepal. The time passed reasonably quickly and almost before I knew it we had landed. There was the usual long wait to collect baggage and for customs and immigration control. Then, another problem arose! I was not allowed into the arrivals lounge as I couldn't find my baggage card and had to wait until everyone else on my flight had left before I was able to collect my luggage and get through, nearly an hour after landing but at last I had arrived safely for the next stage of my adventure and whatever other problems which might arise?

Part 2
NEPAL

1
TLM Hospital, Anandaban

The Leprosy Mission Driver who was to take me to the hospital at Anandaban had been waiting patiently for about two hours but welcomed me warmly with a beaming smile and the national, all occasions, greeting that I was soon to become very familiar with, "Namaste." "Welcome to Nepal Mr. James."

With my luggage safely stored on the back seat of his van and with me sitting alongside him up front, we quickly made our way out of the airport car park and then slowly, very slowly, along the very busy main road. It was packed with people in and on all kinds of vehicles, both modern and ancient, many of which seemed quite un-roadworthy. There were even families on motor scooters, father driving, mum seated behind clutching babies or young children between them and not a safety helmet in sight.

The road itself was in the process of being widened which meant that on the side next to me, was a drop of about a metre with construction vehicles, workmen and pedestrians everywhere with, seemingly, no idea of any order whatsoever. It was as bad, if not worse than the some of the rural roads I had experienced in India.

Progress was very slow, especially through the centre of Kathmandu, Nepal's capital city, a place thronged with traffic of all descriptions, people of all ages moving dangerously in and out of the traffic and tradesmens' wares spilling onto the road itself. It was a wonderful scene of cheerful, colourful, noisy chaos. Indeed yet another 'Welcome to Nepal'. Out of the City along dusty, pock-marked roads, through small pockets of villages, climbing slowly upwards and surrounded on each side by wonderful mountain scenery, until some forty-five minutes after leaving the airport we reached Ananbadan Hospital.

Anandaban Hospital, Nepal

Set high up on the hillside, (I should have realised by now, everything in Nepal is perched on a hillside!), was The Leprosy Mission hospital which was to be my home for the next three days. I was shown to the 'guest house', a substantial brick built property set down and away from the main hospital buildings by some one hundred steps, which I was soon to discover, were to be ever present during my time in Nepal.

My room was basic but very nice. Two beds and lovely thick, warm, fleece blankets which were to become most welcome as it gets very cold at night in the mountains.

Outside on the landing was a shower room and toilet which was to be shared with the other guests, three ladies. It had the old cowboy saloon, swing, type doors with no lock, so it was suggested that I should sing whenever I was in there. I didn't mind doing that but felt sorry for those who had to listen. Still, I suppose that was better than the possible embarrassing alternative!

After a refreshing shower and shave and changing into fresh clothing, I went down to supper and to meet my fellow house guests. They were three young ladies, two from England and the other from the Netherlands. One was a training to become a doctor and the others were nurses.

They had been at the hospital for the last four weeks, experiencing the medical and surgical work with leprosy patients. As I had been delayed at the airport, my supper had gone cold but nevertheless was very welcome. The girls had waited until I arrived to invite me to go with them to the nightly prayer service.

After I had finished my supper we climbed up the one hundred steps to the main hospital building and then another one hundred plus steps to the small chapel where the evening service had started some three quarters of an hour earlier. Of course all the prayers were in Nepalese but it was lovely just to sit quietly and immerse myself in my own quiet prayers of thanksgiving for all the support I had received to get me this far and to be kept safe on the rest of my travels. At the end of the service, I was introduced, welcomed and presented with a small bunch of local flowers which had been freshly picked earlier that day. I responded, with the help of an interpreter, telling them why I was there and giving greetings from The Leprosy Mission, England and Wales and also from the church fellowship at Albany Road Baptist Church, Cardiff.

Anandaban

Back down all those steps to the Guest House where I sat chatting to the girls over a nice cup of tea, listening to what they had been doing and telling them about The Rainbow of Hope and how I was involved with TLM. Then off to my room to spend a short time bringing my journal up to date and prayers.

The prospect of bed was greatly appealing as I was very tired, having had only brief snatches of sleep since waking in my own bed some twenty one hours ago. I was really looking forward to a good sleep and seeing what tomorrow will bring.

2
Hospital Ward Rounds

I woke early, 7.00am. I must have had a reasonable sleep as I couldn't remember waking during the night. A quick shower, not forgetting to sing, before breakfast and on to morning prayers with the girls and TLM staff. The whole ethos of the work of TLM is care and service in God's name and each day started and finished with prayer, which I found to be both calming and inspiring as did, I am sure, all the staff. After the prayer service, I was taken to meet the Hospital Administrator, Mr. Adhikari for a tour of the hospital and the rest of the premises. As well as dealing primarily with those suffering with leprosy, the hospital also serves the local community in general heath, emergency and maternity matters.

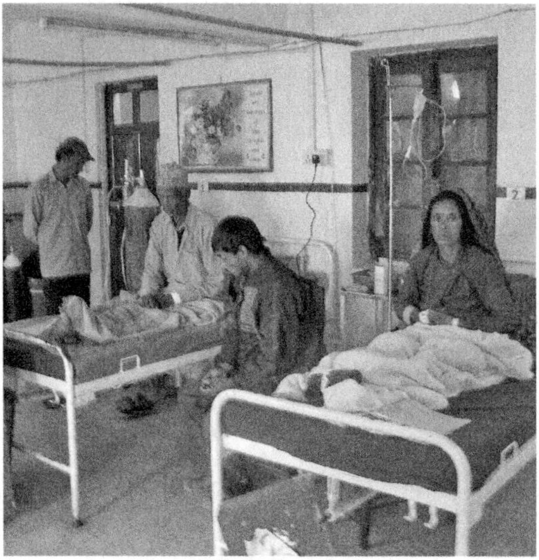

Hospital wards

We visited the various wards, full of patients suffering from the effects of leprosy. Patients with clawed hands; dropped feet; deformed fingers and toes and those with eye problems and open ulcers. There were many who had undergone amputations of fingers, toes and even arms or legs; all in different stages of recovery, physiotherapy or being fitted with prosthetics and learning how to use their new limbs and even being taught the basics of how to bathe and care for their ulcers.

The various clinics and rooms for treatment and rehabilitation were, like the rest of the hospital wards, sparse but functional, brightened only by having been given names, such as Hope, Love, Faith and Peace. This last clinic, named after the nurse working there, looked after patients, mainly young men and boys who, after being prescribed a course of Multi Drug Therapy (MDT) to cure or arrest leprosy, had suffered a reaction to the treatment and had to take a daily course of different medication to combat the reaction.

During my visit of the wards I was introduced to a twenty six year old young lady, Parbati, who, with the help of an interpreter, told me her story. She had been living with her family in a remote village in the far western region of Nepal when at the age of thirteen she began to show the first signs of leprosy although neither she nor her parents were aware of what was it was at the time.

Ashamed of her appearance and fearing her community's reaction, her parents kept her away from school and kept her indoors out of sight. The cause of her condition remained undiagnosed until a TLM community worker, looking for people with leprosy in the area, visited her home and immediately recognised the tell-tale symptoms and quickly did a screening test which confirmed that she did have leprosy. Parbati was accepted as a patient at Anandaban but it was too late to save her toes and some of her fingers which had to be amputated.

Parbita

Having missed much of her school years she is illiterate and is being taught basic reading and arithmetic skills and is slowly beginning to take the first steps of learning to write, despite her deformed hands. She hopes that one day she may be able to earn some money by selling cosmetics but in the meantime is happy living in the hospital, which she now considers to be her home.

On a subsequent visit to the hospital in 2016, she was not there, and upon enquiring after her, I was told that she had improved considerably and has now settled back in her home village some two days travel away in the North West of Nepal. Although still handicapped by the loss of some of her fingers and toes, she is happily running her small, successful cosmetics business which provides her an income and, just as importantly, gives her the huge benefit of confidence and self esteem. Like many other former patients, helped physically and educationally at TLM's hospitals, Parbati, sings the praises of what has been done for her by all the staff at the hospital, in and through the Christian love and healing that she found there. Praise be to God.

3
Telephone Calls To Home

A lovely and perhaps necessary, feature of the hospital is that while all the medical treatment and aftercare is undertaken by the doctors and nursing staff, the patients' personal needs are cared for by their family members who spend a great deal of time on the wards with their sick, loved ones.

With my tour of the wards over, I went back to the Guest House for lunch. I was on my own, as the girls had gone with Dr. Indra and some nurses to TLM's clinic in Patan, one of the outlying areas of Kathmandu where there is a clinic for follow up examinations of surgery, the renewal of dressings and possible changes of medication all to save patients having to come back to the hospital.

As I had a free afternoon I sat in the garden for a short time enjoying the warm sunshine while bringing my journal up to date. Going back over my adventure so far made me think of home so I telephoned Elizabeth (8.00pm in Cardiff). We enjoyed a long chat, catching up but agreed that we would only text each other from now on as telephone calls cost £1.50 per minute, an expensive indulgence.

Everything OK at home, with lots of people praying for me, which served to remind me of why I was here and what my Trek was really about. Sitting in the sunshine was wasted time so I decided to acclimatise myself for what lay ahead by going for a walk. I went down the very steep road from the hospital to the main road. It took me nearly an hour, which in very hot sunshine was a struggle but after a short rest I walked back to the hospital and a comfortable chair in the coolness of the Guest House and a refreshing cup of tea.

This short, two hour stroll gave me some idea of the difficulties I would have to face in the coming days. Having rested, I began to feel rather guilty about just sitting around in the shade, after all this is not supposed to be a holiday, so I decided to do the same walk again, this time attempting to go faster without having taken a rest at the main road. It was somewhat cooler now and it was still a struggle but I made it and, feeling rather smug, I thought, 'this must be doing me some good'!

Hot and sticky after my exertions, I treated myself to a nice shower and even though the girls were not around, sang as loudly as I could belting out some good old songs of praise and worship which made me feel much better.

Refreshed and with fresh, clean clothes I went back into the garden, reading and thinking of what was to come, while I waited for the girls to return from the clinic and our evening meal.

We decided to not attend the evening service and just sat and chatted about our lives and the reasons we were at Anandaban. They were there of course to further their medical training and I was able to witness and to tell them about my involvement with TLM and the Rainbow of Hope. They listened with interest and asked many questions about the work of my two charities and what I was hoping to achieve by undertaking my 'Trek of Hope'.

Two of the girls were leaving for home the next afternoon and so we went to our rooms, relatively early, but I was determined not to go to sleep too soon.

However, after spending some time reading, I began to feel very tired and gave in to a hoped for relaxed slumber.

4
Operations, Guinea Pigs and Mice

Despite going to bed early, I didn't sleep very well, waking every hour or so until I eventually got up at 6.00am. After breakfast we all went to the morning service in the hospital chapel where we met Dr. Indra who invited the Dutch nurse, Lisbeth and I to attend his morning surgery while the other two girls worked on their ward rounds.

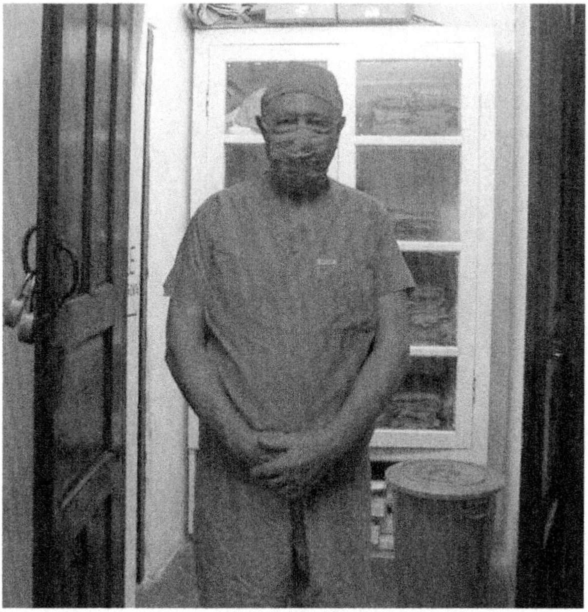

'Doctor' Michael

When we got to the operating theatre we were asked to dress up in 'scrubs' and prepare ourselves by 'scrubbing up', as we would actually be alongside Dr. Indra and his surgical team while he carried out an operation to straighten the clawed hand of an 80 year old leprosy sufferer. It was amazing to see this delicate operation at close quarters and to be allowed to take photographs of the surgeon at work.

It was indeed an honour for me to see something that I had read and heard about and I will now be able, when asked, to explain how this is done. Following the surgery, the patient will undergo about six months physiotherapy, after which time his, now straightened hand, will be able to be used normally again and, furthermore the new physical appearance of his hand will remove the stigma of leprosy. Two huge bonuses.

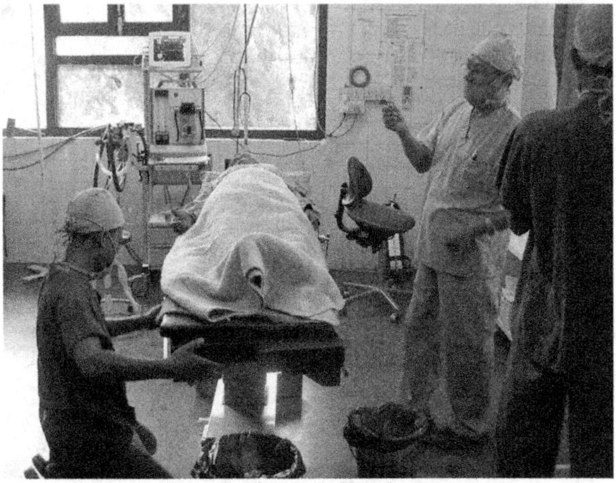

Preparing for clawed hand surgery

That afternoon I had been invited to visit the microbiology laboratories where all the tests and research work are being done into the causes and effects of leprosy, as well of course, of trying to discover a vaccination to cure the disease. The head of the research team was an American scientist, Deanna, who kindly took some time out of her busy day to show me around and explain what she and her team were doing.

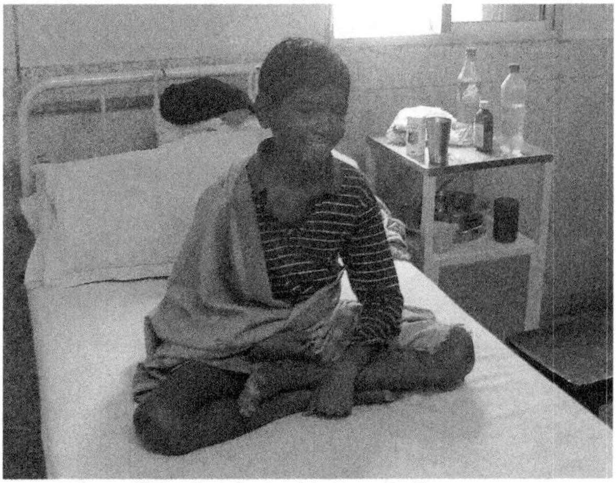

Young boy, having been cured of leprosy

Unfortunately my understanding of the complex technology which goes into their research was pretty limited, so all I can remember is that it involved guinea pigs and white mice, lots and lots of them. A constant supply is needed even though the mice produce a new litter every three weeks. The colony grows rapidly and has to be completely renewed every five years, supplied from a breeding farm in Lucknow, India. I didn't really like to ask what happened to the mice and guinea pigs during the research but I fervently pray that the work being carried out by Deanna and her team will be successful in their quest to find a vaccine to cure leprosy in the near future!

My tour of the laboratories over and with nothing planned for the rest of the day, I decided to go walking again, this time being a little more adventurous.

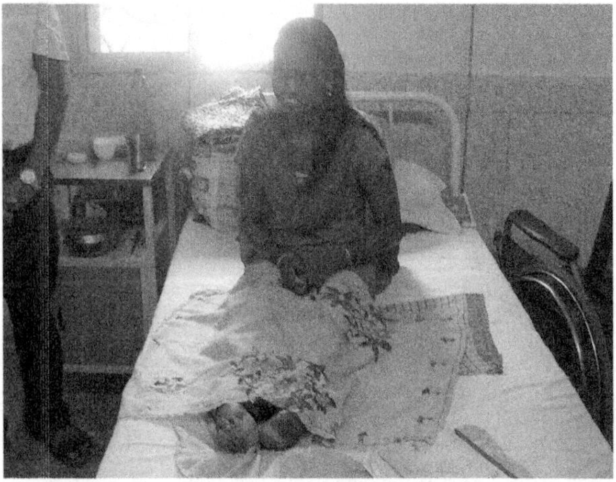

Lovely needlework, despite suffering from leprosy

I climbed back down the steep hill to the main road and then across a river to a little village I could see high up on the hillside. After a long steady, slow climb of about two hours I arrived at a small, pretty group of stone built, zinc sheeted roofs, single storey houses and not a person in sight, only dogs, goats and donkeys all lying down in the shade and completely ignoring this silly old man who had chosen to wander about in the heat of the afternoon.

Taking my cue from the animals, I found a low, flat wall to sit on and drink my water and after a short time decided to lay down to rest. I must have slept for a time and woke to find a young lad of about 5 or 6 years of age looking at me with some curiosity. Seeing me wake, he must have decided that I was in distress because he turned and ran into one of the nearby houses only to return, almost immediately with his Mother. In very broken English and with hand gestures, she asked if I was OK and kindly invited me into her home to take a drink, which I declined.

This seems to have been rather ungracious of me but I reasoned that I might not be welcomed if, when asked, I tried to explain that I was staying at the nearby Leprosy Mission hospital, such is the stigma of the disease among many people. (How quickly I forgot my experience on the train a few years earlier.) Also, by pointing at my watch and with hand movements, I tried to explain that I had to return before it became dark.

There followed another three and a half hours walk before I arrived back at the Guest House in time for a quick shower before supper. There was only Beth and I now as the other two girls had left to fly back home. Supper over, we climbed back up the two hundred steps to the little chapel to attend the evening prayers, then early to bed for my last night as I leave Anandaban tomorrow to meet up with my fellow trekkers in Kathmandu.

My prayers that night were for the on-going work of TLM and thanks for the way in which I had been so graciously received by all I had met, both patients and staff, who were grateful in what I was trying to achieve by undertaking my Trek.

Guest house before and after earthquake

5
Kathmandu

My last morning at Anandaban was, by now, the usual pattern of breakfast, followed by going with Beth to the morning service of prayers and worship but whereas my mornings had been usually busy, nothing had been planned for me today. Nothing to do except to finish my packing and just reflect on my time at the hospital and all I had seen of the dreadful effect of leprosy on those suffering with the disease and their stories of how it had blighted their lives.

However, to counter balance these horrors, was the wonderful way their lives had been changed by the sheer weight of the love, care and medical treatment they had been given by all those at the hospital who served their needs by God given skills and devotion to those who were suffering. To see this work in action was humbling and I felt greatly blessed to have been given the chance to truly witness all that was being done in His Name.

Having said my goodbyes to everyone, I set off for Kathmandu travelling with Dr. Indra and three nurses who were travelling to the hospital's out patients clinic in Patan on the outskirts of the City. Then back into the noisy, colourful, crowded streets of Kathmandu where it took my driver some time to find my hotel, the Hotel Tibet International, which, despite it's rather faded facade, is an extremely nice, comfortable, modern four star hotel with good facilities.

After checking in, I caught the lift to the sixth floor where the hotel's restaurant opened out onto a lovely roof top dining area and where I was to meet up with the others in the trekking party. There to greet me was our expedition leader, Dawa Geljen Sherpa, with two of his colleagues and, a short time later, the other trekkers arrived. Formal introductions over, our group of twelve, consisted of a party of eight, John, Hugh, Shelia, Andy, Steve, Chris, Grace and Dani, all supporting the Yorkshire Cancer Centre, based at St. James' Hospital in Leeds and four others, including me, travelling as individuals. As well as myself, the three others were, another Steve, Jeff and Sarah, each respectively supporting, The Air Ambulance Service, a London based Cancer charity and BEAT, an eating disorder charity.

It always surprises me and, as a Christian it really shouldn't, how many times the number twelve (as in the number of Disciples) keeps cropping up in many of the things I am involved with. It surely is not coincidental and always gives me a feeling of great comfort. It is as if confirmation that God is watching over me and, on this occasion, perhaps more than ever before, I need to be reassured and feel His presence in the days that lie ahead.

Dawa gave us a detailed briefing of what we were likely to encounter on our trek, which on the face of it, was more or less what I expected. Little did I know that it would put me into difficulties that were far more demanding than I could have possibly imagined.

We were issued with individual trek bags which contained a 'mummy' style, winter sleeping bag and heavily quilted, waterproof jacket because, it becomes very cold at night in the Himalayas, even at relatively lower levels of the mountains. It was explained that we were to be allowed only enough clothes and equipment for the period of the trek so as to minimise the loads the porters were to carry and we would be carrying our own rucksacks, or day bags, containing our essential items. The rest of our clothes and personal luggage were to be left at the hotel until our return.

I discovered that I had been teamed to share accommodation with John, who was two years older than me at 77 years of age but much fitter. He was a very experienced trekker, having completed charity walks to Machu Picchu in Peru and the Great Wall of China, as well as covering many parts of the U.K. A great role model for me to follow.

6
A Prayerful Step of Faith

After a short time to ourselves to sort out what we were to take with us or to leave behind, we all met up again to be taken by Dawa on a short tour of the Boudha area of Kathmandu, visiting the local market surrounding a large, Buddhist temple, the Boudhanath Stupa. This impressively ornate temple which totally dominated the market area, was the main attraction to the Buddhist faithful and tourists alike and was festooned with Nepalese prayer flags, which I was to encounter everywhere I travelled in Nepal.

These small linen prayer flags consisting of five colours which represent the Earth (Yellow), Water (Green), Fire (Red), Air/Cloud (White) and Sky/Space (Blue), are hung, continually repeated, in the same sequence and bear the same prayer on the same coloured flag. The flags do not carry prayers to the gods, as one might think, rather that the prayers which promote peace, compassion, strength and wisdom, will be blown on the wind to spread into all pervading space.

Our short tour finished, we went to have supper in a local restaurant just off the market square. When we had settled around the table I was a little surprised and troubled to see that nearly all the waiters were people of restricted height. I asked Dawa about it and he explained that the owners were giving them an opportunity for employment rather than using their staff as a gimmick to attract dinners. I accepted this explanation at it's face value as, indeed all the staff seemed to be very happy.

Prior to commencing our meal I took the opportunity to introduce myself to my new found fellow trekkers. I uttered a quick silent prayer, took a deep breath and boldly stated that I was a Christian and that the purpose of me undertaking the trek was to raise awareness of and funding for, the work of The Leprosy Mission and Rainbow of Hope. Without waiting for comment, I went on to ask if I could say grace before we started our meal, followed by a short prayer for the safe outcome of the trek and the successful sponsorship of all our charities.

This was greeted with complete silence! You could have heard a pin drop! Then one of the young girls cheerfully cried out, "Yeah, go for it!" which of course I was more than pleased to do.

After dinner, we walked back to our hotel through the still crowded streets which were now ablaze with many lights and the competing sounds of a mixture of Nepalese, Indian and Western music. Dawa then gave us another briefing, mainly to stress about curtailing our amounts of luggage as each of the porters would be carrying two 40lbs bags (36.20kg). Then off to bed at about 10.30pm. John was almost immediately asleep but my head was full of the day(s) ahead and my prayers that night were for my fellow travellers and myself to be granted the strength to complete the task to which we had committed ourselves and I struggled to get to sleep despite having to rise at 5.30am the next day.

7
Starting Off. Another Step of Faith

I woke on and off during the night and eventually rose at 5.00 am. fully awake. I had a hot shower, making the most of it, anticipating that it could be at least another week before I returned to such luxury and then made John and I a cup of tea.

Breakfast, with the others in the already warm sunshine was taken on the roof top dining area where we enjoyed a lovely Nepalese version of a, 'full English breakfast'. Quite a lot of excited chatter among us before boarding a mini bus to Kathmandu airport for our 8.30am flight to Pokhara. Despite being fully awake earlier, I was now starting to feel tired. Early mornings are not usual for me but I had better start getting used to them as they will become commonplace during the trek.

The small airport was full of people, all seemingly going trekking to different parts on Nepal. I was amused to see that we were flying with 'Yeti Airlines', an appropriate name for being in the Himalayas but I hoped, it would be the only Yeti we would encounter on our travels.

The plane was small, seating only 30 people but perfectly adequate for our half hour flight to Pokhara and the start of our great adventure. We arrived safely and quickly cleared the airport building and out to a mixture of a mini bus and two cars to accommodate our party and luggage to take us to our stating point into the mountains at Nayapul, some 1,070 metres (3,500 feet) above sea level.

The two-hour journey over increasingly rough roads, heavily trafficked with many kinds of vehicles, all intent on overtaking the vehicle in front, often on blind bends and with a steep drop into the valley below, was quite a hair raising experience. The drive took us ever higher and deeper into the mountains and gave us a small sample of the scale of the land, which was only the foothills of the majestic mountains, the Himalayas.

Walking bushes, with smiles

Reaching Nayapul, we disembarked from our vehicles to be introduced to our trek doctor, to be known hereafter as 'The Doc', four guides and the six porters who were to carry all our equipment. Each porter was to carry two bags, each weighing 40lbs, tied together and carried on their backs and supported with straps around their waists and around their foreheads.

As well as the official trek doctor, there were

two other doctors among the Yorkshire contingent of our group so we should be OK for any health problems which might arise on our journey.

Our Trek started off at 11.30am and this was when, for the first time, it hit me.

"What have I let myself in for?" "Why am I doing this?"

"Yes, I must be crazy!"

More smiles

For all the years I had thought about this moment, all the planning, training and worrying about getting sponsorship, all the difficulties and obstacles I had overcome to get to this point, and even with some vague sense how physical it would be, were all now a lifetime away, another country, another part of my world. This was it! No turning back now!

Seeing my fellow travellers striding out, excitedly and confidently in front of me, I was overcome by a sense of, not fear but the realisation that

I may have bitten off more than I could chew. Then as I always do at times of uncertainty, I turned to God in silent prayer.

"Father God. I have listened to your constant, quiet, small voice saying, "Michael, this is what I want you to do for Me."

"Lord, if I have heard You correctly and it is Your Will, please let me feel Your presence and, in Your strength, allow me to complete whatever lies before me."

Leaving my prayers with God and taking a deep breath, I hurried off to catch up with my trekking partners.

Starting off

We walked through numerous little villages and

up through increasingly steep countryside until we came to a narrow, steel and wooden bridge over a fast flowing, river which we had to cross. Rather surprisingly I then discovered that I was not the only one in the party who had fears. One or two of the group had to be persuaded and helped across the bridge and, I must admit, I felt better from having the knowledge that we all face individual challenges and fears in our lives.

Bridge of others' fears

Safely across, we came to the small village of Modi Khola Bridge where we stopped for lunch, which was very welcome, having not eaten since breakfast, some six hours earlier. After a good meal, two big cups of tea and a rest, I began to relax and thought that things might not be too bad after all.

How wrong could I be? After lunch, we started off again and this is when things began to get harder. A steady uphill climb, along a narrow, rough track which contained many steps made of natural stone. Not all of the stone steps were of regular shape or size which made walking difficult. There were some shallow steps, some deeper steps and not laid in a uniform level. The climb got steeper and steeper and with three long rest stops, we took about three hours to reach our overnight stop at the little village of Syauli Bazar - 1,220 metres (4,003 feet).

First of many thousands of steps

The final steep section of our climb was made even more difficult because the last hour was undertaken in pouring rain which, apart from getting us soaked, made the already awkward steps even more treacherous because of the rain mixing with the animal waste, which in many places covered the steps, making them very slippery underfoot. All in all, I was really struggling and this was only the first day.

I must confess that at our hotel in Kathmandu, prior to starting the Trek, I had been somewhat disappointed to learn that we were not going to be sleeping in tents as I had wanted to experience 'roughing it' but with the now, torrential rain, I was very pleased to be staying in a Nepalese 'Tea House' or small hotel.

More steps

These hotels are built mainly of plywood, with walls which shook alarmingly every time someone passed by our bedrooms. The rooms themselves were pretty small and basic, with hard wooden beds and very, very thin mattresses, no more than one inch thick, which I was to discover really didn't matter because I would be able go to sleep fast on almost any kind of surface after a hard day's trek.

After a good, substantial supper, it was suggested that went to bed at 9.00pm. as we had been awake since 5.00am. and we have an early start tomorrow with another long day ahead of us. Dawa has told us that we face the frightening prospect of having to climb some fourteen thousand of the uneven stone steps. I find that very difficult to contemplate and I wonder, hope even, that he is joking.

Today has been very hard for me and my prayers are those of thanksgiving to God, for having brought me and my fellow trekkers safely through this day.

8
The 14,000 Steps

Despite being very tired, I didn't sleep very well, although that is generally the norm for me as I get older. I was awake at midnight and again at 3.00am, needing the toilet, which proved to be another adventure.

The only toilet was at the far end of our corridor. With no lights at that time in the morning, to save the generators, I had to feel my way to the bedroom door and into the pitch blackness that enveloped the building, inching my way along the walls of the corridor until I came to the toilet.

Thank goodness it was unoccupied!. Then back along the same route to the bedroom. I resolved that the next night I would equip myself with my head torch if I needed a visit to the toilet. Safely back in bed, I slept soundly until John woke me at 5.45am.

There was a long queue to get into the wash room for a cold shower. Then breakfast before setting off on the next leg of our journey from Syauli Bazar to Ghandruk - 1,940 metres (6,364 feet). Dawa once again warned us about the 14,000 steps we would encounter on today's climb. Surely he was just teasing us, wasn't he ? No, he wasn't! Having completed the climb, all I can say is that whoever counted them got it wrong. There must have been three times as many! But I must not get ahead of myself, as we hadn't even set off yet.

With our porters, carrying their heavy loads, starting off ahead of us, we began to climb, almost immediately up a quite steep incline and the start of the numerous, uneven, stone steps. I found the first part to be very difficult and it was to get progressively worse.

After the first thirty minutes I needed to pause to catch my breath every ten minutes or so and that was just the start of the day.

Our faithful porters

Increasingly, I found myself stopping to take a drink of water and spend some time looking at or photographing the magnificent scenery which was all around us, while all the time trying to catch my breath.

This had it's benefits though because as well as enjoying the rests, the scenery was wonderful, much of which I would have missed by just plodding along with my head down.

I was to find each day would become more difficult with the numerous stone steps disappearing seemingly ever upward and my progress becoming slower and slower with me having to stop at regular intervals to rest and drink.

During my many stops, there were a number of

occasions when I was passed by groups of younger trekkers coming down the mountain on an alternative direction to our route.

Seeing me sitting there, probably looking exhausted, they inevitably would stop and smile, ask if I was OK and enquire about my age.

My reply, that I was 75 years old, was always greeted by incredulous cries of, "How old?" generally followed by a request to have a 'selfie', taken with me.

There must be many photographs of a silly old man circulating on social media throughout South East Asia. As most of these young people were Japanese, Chinese or Indians, they respected my great age and instead of the usual cry of, "You must be crazy!" they seemed genuinely pleased that I was attempting the same difficult trek as they were. These brief encounters were most encouraging and lifted my spirit and with yet another silent prayer I was able to press on again until the next much needed stop. The only problem with these regular stops was that I was worrying that I was delaying the others. Because of the difficulty of the climb, today was scheduled to be a half day trek, albeit, of some six hours, with lunch. Then a free afternoon when we could spend some time in the local village of Ghandruk which was to be our overnight stop and gave us an opportunity to visit the small monastery and a museum of Nepalese life.

Some of the younger, fitter members of our group arrived at the lunch break on time, while others drifted in at different later times, except for me, arriving a good forty five minutes later to a very generous, warm and encouraging applause. Being supported and encouraged by Dawa and one of the younger guides,

Ang Dandi Sherpa, who stayed with me to ensure that I was OK, was reassuringly welcome.

A welcome lunch

From then on Dandi was assigned to be my personal guide, offering to carry my back pack for me, which was a great help and he even found me a small shop where I enjoyed a welcome rest while drinking a large mug of hot, milky, coffee. Lovely!

The information we had been given prior to signing up for the Trek was that, it was not to be a race. The pace would be decided by the slowest member of the party (on this trek, me!) and I found that to be very much the case.

Nobody commented about my coming in last on each leg of the climb. They appreciated my effort and warmly welcomed my arrival, even joking that while waiting for me they were able to enjoy an extra time of rest and another beer. I was glad somebody had benefited!

It got very cold in the evenings and at night when the pock filled jackets and sleeping bags we had been given became very welcome. During the day it was very hot, often reaching 34 degrees and the thinness of the air at high altitudes made it seem much hotter, especially in direct sunlight. This meant that we had to keep drinking the four litres of boiled water which had been provided for us at the start of each day.

On this particular day, I had drunk all my water so when I eventually arrived at Ghandruk, my mouth was so dry that I could not open it to speak but a large bottle of refreshing cold beer soon improved things and enabled me to enjoy my very welcome lunch and I soon relaxed.

After lunch and before our 'free' afternoon, the 'The Doc', wanted to carry out individual tests on each of us to see how we were coping. Being rather concerned about my own efforts that day, I volunteered to go first. He checked my blood pressure (120/70) and heart rate, which were both OK and said that I was generally pretty good after my day's exertions and, better still, said that I was well enough to continue the Trek, which was the news that I wanted to hear.

9
'Different Faiths, No Faith and Togetherness'

Having a 'free' afternoon was just what I needed after what probably was, the most physical day that I have ever encountered. There were times on the climb that morning when I really didn't think that I could carry on. Although each stop was welcome, the sight of yet more steps disappearing into in the distance had me quietly praying, "Please God, not again!" The strange thing was, that after a leisurely lunch, followed by a refreshing cold shower; a change of clothes and especially footwear, into sandals and no socks, instead of my thick socks and sturdy walking boots, was just bliss! The fatigue of the day seemed to have just melted away. My difficulties for the moment were put aside, God had given me the strength to make it and I had no thoughts nor worries of what may lay before me the next day. Together with the rest of the group, I took a short walk to the small, local village. There we visited a museum which housed an exhibition of the, mainly pictorial, history of the village and its surrounding area and, of course, like in many of our own museums, we had to pass though a gift shop on our way out. This housed many items of woollen shawls and hats made by the local people and the shopkeeper persuaded two of our group to dress in traditional wedding garb. This they were happy to do but were then surprised to be asked to pay a small amount for each item worn. As this was a way of preserving the museum and provide a small income to the monks, we all contributed to the fund.

The monastery, although in itself relatively

small, dominated all the other buildings in the area and was dedicated to the Guran Faith. Nepal has some sixty ethnic groups and an estimated ninety different dialects. It also has two main faiths, Hinduism and Buddhism, with other beliefs, such as Christian and Muslim in smaller numbers and the Guran Faith is just one of the many other smaller faiths.

Nepali prayer flags

It was a pleasant afternoon which afforded us some time to get to know each other a little better and chat about our families, jobs, hobbies and our individual reasons for coming on the Trek and the different charities we were supporting. What was very pleasing to me was, even without me raising the subject, a number of the group easily shared with me that they believed in God and had been brought up on Christian principles. Although only one or two still attended church most of the group were no longer, 'church goers', except at weddings and funerals.

Nevertheless they were polite and gracious enough to ask about my Church and the work we do in our local community and about the two Christian charities I was supporting by doing the Trek.

I also enquired about their charities and why they had decided to undertake the Trek and soon discovered that whilst they might choose not to call themselves, 'practising Christians', their basic principles had a strong Christian ethos, as in caring for and wanting to help and serve others.

Eight of our group were supporting the Yorkshire Cancer Centre. Of the other three members, one was supporting a London based cancer charity, another was supporting The Air Ambulance Service and the third was supporting a charity named BEAT which helps people with eating disorders.

The twelve of us were becoming quite a close knit unit. Each struggling with the difficulties of the Trek in his or her own way whilst completely caring for, encouraging and supporting each other, helped of course, in no small way by our leader, Dawa, 'The Doc', our guides and porters. They saw to our every need, preparing the way ahead and making sure that at least one of them, in my case, Dandi, stayed with those who were struggling, without any word or sign of irritation or frustration at the slowness of our progress.

We were all of different faiths or of no faith but our togetherness was total. We were indeed truly blessed. Thanks be to God!

I don't know if it was because I had been talking about my family but I suddenly had the urge to contact home. It had been three days since my last text message and the higher we were getting into the mountains there seemed to be less and less of a chance of getting a mobile phone signal.

After supper I tried again, this time lucky enough to get a telephone call through just as my family were finishing their Sunday lunch After a week of having curry in some form or other for breakfast, lunch and supper, I could almost smell the roast beef but this lovely image was immediately overtaken by being able to have a long chat with my wife and daughter. An expensive call but well worth it! It was good to hear their voices and I went to bed happy with, once again, prayers of grateful thanks on my lips.

10
Mountain Views and a Birthday Party

Our guides woke us at 5.30am. wanting us to see a beautiful sunrise over the mountains, especially Annapurna South and Machapuchhre, better known as 'the Fishtail' because it's twin peaks resemble fish tail fins. It really was a wonderful sight and well worth the early wake-up call.

Early morning view of Machapuchre (Fishtail)

Nature, in all its different aspects, is a truly wonderful witness to God's creation.

Today we were to climb a more testing, steep section of almost seven hundred metres from Ghandruk to Tadapani - 2,630 metres (8,630 feet). After breakfast we started off at 7.30am. Almost immediately I began to feel that things were to get more difficult for me, even more than the previous days. Even at that time of morning the sun was very hot. more noticeably so, probably because of the thinner air at that altitude. I really struggled to manage the inevitable stone steps and had to make numerous stops to drink water while admiring the majestic mountain views and to catch my breath. After a hard struggle of nearly five hours, we arrived at our lunch stop by which time we all benefited from the rest as much as from our meal.

A wild strawberry

Then it was on again. This time passing along one of the few shorter, flatter sections of our route, through a large rhododendron forest which gave us welcome shade.

Unfortunately however the trees and bushes had lost all their lovely flower blooms. The rhododendron is the Nepalese national flower and grows abundantly in the mountains but in dense forests of trees rather than the familiar bushes we know in the UK. We continued our climb for another two hours until mid afternoon when we reached our tea house hotel, where we were to have our overnight stop. After waking up at 5.30am and walking for nearly eight hours, I was completely worn out.

Birthday meal: pizza, fries and Mo Mo's

On one of my many stops during the day, Dawa pointed out that I was sitting next to a wild strawberry plant, I really couldn't have cared less about plants at that time but expressed a real interest and even took a photograph of it. Anything to gain more time before continuing! The higher altitude and the heat was making our climb very difficult but thankfully nobody was showing any signs of the thing we all feared most, altitude sickness.

Arriving at our over night stop in mid-afternoon, some of us relaxed until supper but others, the younger and fitter element of our group, went off in search of exotic birds and monkeys to photograph.

Totally spent, I just lay on my bed for a while and then, while waiting for the others to return, I had my first, lukewarm, shower since we left the hotel in Kathmandu. It was barely warm, the chill was just off the water and I had to pay for the pleasure! One Hundred Nepal Rupees (about £0.60) but worth every penny, as, up until then, we had only ice cold washes or showers while on the Trek.

Birthday girl with chocolate birthday cake

Tonight supper was different. It was Sarah's 20th birthday and Dawa had organised a special meal. Not the usual boiled rice with lentil dhal but tomato soup, followed by pizza, fried chow mein and Mo Mo's, which are delicious Nepalese steamed dumplings filled with some kind of minced meat, and all washed down with refreshingly cold Everest or Gorka beer. This was followed by a large, chocolate birthday cake which had been made at our previous overnight stop and carried in a cool box all day, by one of our guides.

A lovely touch and a welcome surprise at the end of a difficult day.

I was in bed again by 8.00pm with yet more prayers of thanksgiving for surviving the day and in preparation for yet another early start tomorrow but, rather surprisingly, with no real fears or concerns about what might lay ahead.

11
'Fizzy Drinks and Chocolate Bars'

As anticipated, another early call, 5.30 am. The inevitable cold shower followed by breakfast and the promise of another long climb, this time from Tadapani - 2,630 metres (8,630) feet to Ghorepani - 2,860 metres (9,383 feet). Not too far in terms of altitude but once again up the now inevitable, difficult stone steps. Dawa had not mentioned how many there were to be this time and I think we were all afraid to ask. It seemed ominous!

The only steps with handrails

Almost immediately the steepness of the climb was apparent, almost vertical. I found it very difficult, having to take the steep, uneven steps, one at a time rather than just striding out. This, together with having to stop for breath and to take on water at increasingly more frequent intervals, made for very slow going by me with the others, spread out at different distances from each other, climbing on ahead.

Dawa was obviously concerned with my slow progress and encouraged me by supplying a bottle of Coke Cola and a Mars bar (surprisingly both readily available in these remote areas). These were very welcome to boost energy levels but perhaps not in my case with Type 2 Diabetes – too much sugar – not that I even thought about it at the time.

With this boost and with Dawa and Dandi staying with me I eventually made it to our lunch stop about three quarters of an hour behind the others, once again to a round a of encouraging applause.

It had been four and a half hours of a difficult climb in very hot conditions and all I could think about was to sit down in the shade to rest.

Then, without warning, I had to dash into the trees to be violently sick!

After sitting quietly for a short while, I eventually tried to eat something but just couldn't face it. 'The Doc', examined me to check on my condition. My blood pressure was 140/80, slightly higher then yesterday and my oxygen/blood level was 89 which he was satisfied with. He then tested my heart and my breathing which were also OK but he detected a slight, uneven, heart rhythm. We discussed all of what had happened during the day and he came to the conclusion that it wasn't the dreaded 'altitude sickness', which would have meant the end of the Trek for me. Thankfully he decided that after a short rest I would be OK to continue. He thought that it was probably a combination of the long hard climb, the heat of the day and my intake of the chocolate and the Coke Cola, which I rarely ever drink, raising my sugar levels. Never a good thing for a diabetic!

He suggested that I should have a couple of days without, tea, coffee, beer and sugary soft drinks. The thought of a few days drinking only boiled water seemed to be a small price to pay if it allowed me to continue, especially having seen a young Japanese man who was suffering from altitude sickness, being strapped on the back of a donkey to be taken quickly down all those uneven steps to a lower altitude to recover. I was thankful that it wasn't me.

After the examination, I slept for forty five minutes before we set off again. The others had gone on ahead and once again Dawa and Dandi stayed with me. Another long, steep, slow climb of almost five hours with me making numerous stops before we reached our overnight stop.

This last stretch of the climb was a very difficult time for me and I really struggled to set off again after each short stop but I was determined to make it and was very glad to eventually get there. A cold, refreshing shower, then supper but I was so exhausted, I could only eat a little and went to bed early. I couldn't sleep but just to lie there, relaxing, was just what I needed after a long, steep climb of nearly nine hours.

In one way or another, a very eventful day. Once again, my prayers were of thanksgiving and a request for continued strength to face what was to be the highlight, or perhaps I should I say, the highest point, of the Trek. Poon Hill!

12
'Poon Hill'

Poon Hill. I had read and thought about it from the early days of considering undertaking the Trek and together with the rest of my travelling companions, I was looking forward to it with an equal mixture of excitement and apprehension.

A very early call, this time at 4.00am. A quick wash and a drink of cold, boiled water remembering what 'The Doc', had said yesterday, no caffeine! We were told to put on plenty of layers of clothing, including our warm jackets and waterproof trousers as it would be wet and cold. Sadly, we had our first casualty of the Trek. Dani had badly twisted her ankle on the last stages of yesterday's climb. I had wondered why I hadn't seen her at supper time the previous evening, and I just assumed that, like me, she was exhausted. Apparently her injury was so bad that there was the possibly of her being flown by helicopter to hospital in Kathmandu later that morning.

So, setting off in the dark, with only the light of our head torches picking out our way and the feet of the person directly ahead of us, we climbed the very steep stone steps, almost as steep as a staircase. As we climbed and during my many stops, I became aware of other trekkers on the same route. Normally there was just our little group on our daily climbs but now there was a constant stream of people all heading the same way. Who were they and where had they all come from? After nearly two hours we eventually reached our goal, the summit of Poon Hill. We (I) had made it!

Poon Hill – 'We made it!'

Poon Hill – 'Where did they all come from?'

Poon Hill – 'The doc'

Poon Hill – proudly supporting our charities

Poon Hill. Standing at 3,210metres, (10,500feet) above sea level, this was the highest I had ever been on my own two feet. It dwarfed my success at scaling Pen Y Fan which, at only 886 metres, is merely a small hill.

I became overwhelmed with a sense of achievement, fatigue and relief and suddenly burst into tears. Yes, I probably was crazy to think that I could do this but YES, I had made it! Thanks be to God.

All of our group were ecstatic and as we hugged each other at our success, to my astonishment I discovered that we were all crying tears of joy and emotion. While we were congratulating each other on our achievement, one of our group said to me, "Michael, I think that this is a good time offer a prayer of thanksgiving." This brought me to tears again and to my everlasting shame, I quietly declined, saying that I was far too emotional to pray coherently and, as Dani was not with us, I would pray when we were all together later that morning at breakfast.

We had made a very early start to the day so as to catch the wonderful sunrise that usually presented itself at this time of the morning, 6.00am. but not today. Because of the cloud cover, a rather weak sun briefly showed itself, appearing almost apologetically, though the clouds and quickly hid again. However, it wasn't going to spoil our great achievement and by now it was light enough for us to marvel at the majestic scenery and have a group photograph with all of us proudly wearing our tee-shirts showing the names of the various charities we were supporting.

It also revealed the full extent of the large number of others on the summit. All those who were climbing ahead of us and the many who silently passed me in the dark on their way to the top. There must have been at least two hundred excited trekkers of all nationalities celebrating their own achievement, taking photographs of each other and enjoying the views while resting before setting off back down the mountain.

13
Downhill at Last

For the last four days we had been climbing up the mountains. Up all those many thousands of steps but suddenly we were now going down hill and, if anything this return, two hour stretch from the summit was even more difficult, especially with me now only able to take one step at a time to save putting pressure on my weaker left knee.

Downhill at last and meeting locals on the way

When we eventually arrived back at the tea house we were given confirmation that Dani needed to be flown out to hospital in Kathmandu to assess the extent of her ankle injury and her subsequent treatment.

While we were enjoying our very welcome breakfast, Dawa had been making decisions on what was going to be a long arduous trek to our next overnight stop at Tikedhungga, at 1,520 metres (4,987 feet), a descent of some 1,500 metres (4921 feet) from the summit of Poon Hill. It was agreed that while Dawa, Grace and Steve would wait until the helicopter arrived and seen that Dani was safely on her way, Dandi and I, being the slowest, would set off first with the rest of the group following about thirty minutes behind us.

Dani being helicoptered out

Having said our farewells to Dani, we set off down the mountain. The steep decent was through another section of forest which gave welcome shade from the already hot sun but still with the inevitable, irregular stone steps. How many today I wondered! As I had discovered earlier, going downhill was much more difficult for me and it was very slow going, taking nearly four hours to arrive at our lunch stop and having been passed along the way by the main group.

Dawa had realized that we would not all be together for lunch and had told the others to choose anything we wanted from the rather surprisingly (for a small hut in the middle of nowhere) large and varied menu of pizzas, rice dishes, noodles and different soups. A big change from our usual daily lunch of vegetables, lentil dhal and boiled rice but remembering 'The Doc's advice, I chose not to have a large, rich meal and had just a bowl of muesli with hot milk and a glass of boiled water.

More locals

Having eaten and being suitably rested, Dandi and I once again set off ahead of the others as there was still a long way to go and we didn't want to slow down their progress. After about an hour of a long steep downward stretches, they caught up and passed us, as did Dawa, Grace and Steve about another hour later, having seen Dani settled into the helicopter for the flight to hospital. After numerous stops for water and rests, Dandi pointed to some buildings in the far distance which he indicated was to be our overnight stop. When I asked how long it would take us, he simply pointed at his watch and said, "One hour."

Guitarist to speed us on our way

Encouraged by the knowledge that it would not be too far, I set off with something of a spring in my step, even though it was still only one step at a time. Imagine how I felt some two hours later when we met Dawa coming to see where we were. Something must have been lost in translation between Dandi and I, because when I told Dawa what Dandi had said, he just laughed and said that we still had another hour or so to go but there was another small tea-house at the next village where I could have a rest and a drink. This we did and to make me feel better, I enjoyed a nice mug of hot milky chocolate.

Young girls on their four-hour round trip to school

Before we set off on what I hoped (prayed) would be the last leg of the day, we changed into our waterproofs because it had started raining heavily. We still had some way to go and our progress was made even slower by the rain making the steps of the steep descent very slippery. Indeed, despite my two trusty walking poles, I lost my footing on at least three occasions and fell back heavily on the steps.

Fortunately I suffered no damage but I later found out that Sheila had also taken a tumble which shook her up and she was unable to join us for supper.

At the time that I fell, supper was still a long way off, as was our overnight stop. When Dandi and I eventually arrived at the 'welcome arch' of

Tikhedhungga, we found that, as usual, our accommodation was at the very top end of the little village and it took us another half an hour to get there at precisely 6.00pm. From our very early start that morning until I reached my room, it had been a very long, very hard, downward descent of a fourteen hour day. No wonder I was exhausted and from the lack of the usual welcoming applause of the others who were nowhere to be seen, it would appear that they too had found it hard going.

Me looking worn out, with Sarah, Grace and Steve

However, one good thing was that I managed to get another luke-warm shower to freshen up before supper. I was so tired that I could eat very little food and decided to go to bed early to get some rest before our last day of trekking tomorrow.

Before I left for bed we had been asked to give a donation of £40.00 each as a 'thank you' to our faithful guides and porters, which meant that from this pot of money each of them would each receive a gratuity of £60.00 for the trek.

Dawa, between John and Michael

That only amounted to £10.00 each, per day. Not much to us but they had earned every penny of what was, for them, a doubling of what they usually earned per day. My prayers that night were very much of grateful thanks for the way in which I had been looked after during the very long descent from Poon Hill and although Shelia and I had fallen and all the others were in varying forms of degrees of exhaustion, we were all OK, except of course for Dani, now safely in hospital in Kathmandu but apparently she also was going to be OK.

14
The Last Day of Trekking

Today was to be our last day of trekking and we were granted an extra long lie-in, until 6.00am! Breakfast was an unusually quick one for Dandi and I, as we had been asked to set off before the others to enable us all to arrive in time to catch our pre-arranged transports back to Pokhara.

A happy band of trekkers, with Dawa, Dandi and 'the Doc'

So off we went following the now familiar, steep staircase of stone steps. We travelled for about an hour and suddenly, the trail started to even out more, along ever widening dirt roads suitable for vehicles. This made things much easier for me and also for all the others as they quickly caught up with us. We made steady progress, now walking at a reasonable pace through some really lovely countryside, until after about an hour, we stopped for a rest alongside a wide, wild, fast flowing river. Dawa had decided that after this final rest stop, the main group would set off ahead of me in order to catch their coach at Nayapul for the trip back to Pokhara.

So came the parting of our ways. I had joined the group as an individual, arriving in Kathmandu ahead of them and now they were leaving me behind. We started out as strangers and over the last week in which each of us had faced and overcome our individual difficulties of one kind or another, we had become a very close knit group of people.

A group which had helped and encouraged each other to carry on each day and literally, every 'step' of the many thousands along our way. We all realised how difficult this Trek had been but with the thought of our charities in mind and all those who had sponsored us, we pressed on and, eventually made it.

I decided that this would be the perfect time to voice a prayer of thanksgiving, especially as we were now together for the last time, including 'The Doc.', all our guides, porters and sherpas and of course our chief inspiration, Dawa Sherpa but with the sad exception of Dani who was, thankfully, now well and recovering in the hospital in Kathmandu.

So I prayed. Giving thanks for the way we all got along together; for safely completing the Trek; for our charities and for God being with us, every step of the way. I was overjoyed when my prayer was greeted with loud 'Amens', which was so different to the silence which followed my prayer on that first night at the restaurant in Kathmandu. 'Thanks be to God'.

Everyone came to say their personal goodbyes to me and most of them were as emotional as I was.

‘The Doc’, gave me a final health check. My blood pressure was 139/84. He said that I was OK but suggested that I should see my own doctor when I got back to Cardiff, about the slightly irregular heart beat he had detected when checking me over. This I promised to do.

After numerous team photographs, Dawa gave me my tickets for the flight from Pokhara to Kathmandu where he will meet me again after my short stay at the Raniban Retreat. Then they were off.

Alone now, except for the faithful Dandi, I set off on the last leg of my trek, along the dirt track and with long stretches of the stone steps, until we arrived at the restaurant at Modi Khola Bridge, the same one where we stopped to have lunch on the first day of the Trek. It was very familiar, bringing back my thoughts of that first morning, and very reassuring that we were getting close to the end of the trail. Over a final drink of hot chocolate and a reasonable rest, I tried to make Dandi understand how appreciative I was for his faithfulness in staying with me and especially for his patience in putting up with my slowness, without complaint.

With the lack of language between us I am not sure how much he understood, so I gave him most of the Nepalese Rupees I had left. He was delighted and I subsequently worked out that this amounted to the equivalent of an extra day’s pay for him.

Well worth it for me and so it seemed, for him. Drinks finished we once again crossed the steel and wooden bridge over the wild river and plodded on for the last hour of my Trek, through a number of small villages and with the magnificent sight of the beautiful snow capped mountains, including Annapurna South, until we at last arrived at our starting and finishing point of Nayapul. The others had long gone but I was to travel by taxi with Dandi and one of our other guides to Pokhara, where they both lived and on to my hotel for the next few days.

A long slow drive behind a string of buses and trucks before we reached Pokhara. Dandi and I said our farewells after the adventures we had shared during the trek. No words could be spoken but I am sure that he realised the depth of my appreciation for the way in which he had patiently looked after me on our journey together. He was wonderful and it would have been much more difficult for me without him.

15
More Steps and Two Nights of R+R

I continued in the taxi to my mountain top hotel, the Raniban Retreat, some 115 metres (378 feet) above lake Fewa, a trip that took forty five minutes to the main entrance of the hotel, which I then had to access by climbing some five hundred steps. Yes, more steps!

Fortunately I had been warned of this when I booked the hotel so I was prepared for it and after all the steps of the last six days, I could handle it. However, it was apparently the hotel's policy for clients to have their bags carried up for them by it's 'house boy'.

Eventually the 'boy' came to greet me. He looked even older than me (75) but he easily picked up my heavy bag and practically ran up the five hundred steps with me following a long way behind.

The views from the hotel were wonderful and I was given a warm welcome and an equally welcome long glass of chilled mango juice, which I really enjoyed while relaxing on the hotel patio taking in the beautiful scenery. Then came a heart stopping moment. The receptionist came to inform me that my room had been cancelled. Total shock and horror! After making enquiries, it seemed that as I had booked on-line, I should have confirmed the booking two days prior to my arrival at the hotel. I was not aware of that and anyway, I couldn't receive nor send, any e-mails up in mountains. Fortunately, I was told that the hotel was not fully booked and so I could stay after all. What a relief!

I was given a lovely room with a large patio

door which offered panoramic views over Pokhara and the beautiful Lake Fewa. Just as, or perhaps, even more important, after six days of hard trekking and basic facilities, the room had a big comfortable double bed and a large shower room.

Brilliant! It didn't take me long to get into the shower but much longer to get out of it. The effect of a long, leisurely, hot, shower was wonderful and I took my time over washing my hair and shaving, for the first time in a week.

Climbing back up the steps to the hotel dining room to enjoy a nice Nepalese / Chinese meal before taking a cold banana lassi (an Indian yogurt and fruit drink) out on to the veranda where I was treated to a spectacular lightning storm while waiting for a pre-arranged telephone call from Elizabeth.

It was lovely to hear her voice as we had only been able to exchange short text messages while I was in the mountains. I felt ready to go home but I still had another day of relaxation at Ranaban before flying back to Kathmandu.

Telephone call over, I treated myself to a pot of hot chocolate while watching the spectacular electrical storm rage though the mountains.

Nature in all its aspects is wonderful, as is our God who created it. My prayers that night were a hymn of praise, 'To God be the Glory, great things He has done!'.

16
Farewell to the Mountains

Despite the large, comfortable bed, I didn't sleep well, waking very hour or so before finally getting up at 6.00am.

New habits die hard it would seem! But today was different in so many ways. A long, leisurely, hot shower followed by an equally long time spent over breakfast. It was great not to be rushed in any way, I could do what I liked, my time was my own.

However my problems still hadn't finished. The receptionist asked if I intended to settle my bill with my credit card. Apparently, the storm of the previous night had knocked out the credit/debit card machine, so I was asked could I pay in cash. That would be difficult because I had given most of Nepali currency to Dandi and had very little left but as I was not leaving until the next morning it was decided that I would try to pay later that night or in the morning. Fortunately, after supper that evening the card machine subsequently came back online and so I paid early just in case it crashed again.

Much relieved, I sat out on the hotel's veranda relaxing in a beautiful warm evening with a large pot of delicious Nepali coffee, the first coffee I had since I was taken ill in the mountains.

As I was sitting there the old hotel porter came to say goodnight and to assure me that there would be a good clear view of the Annapurna Mountain range if I got up early the next morning. Before I went off to bed I decided to catch up on filling in my journal, which also gave me time to reflect on all that had happened to me since leaving home. As I read, the memories came flooding back to me.

All the time spent worrying whether I should undertake the Trek. Was it wise for a 75 year old man to attempt it?

Was it just my own wish or was I listening to God speaking to me, prompting me?

I now have no doubt in my mind. It was God. Without a doubt and I really believe that, once I had decided to go, He enabled me to see it through, in His strength.

God was with me, every step of the way and there were many thousands of steps on the Trek. He was also with me before I left home, helping me overcome all the obstacles, (logistical steps) I faced that were put in my way before I even reached Nepal. All my worries about those problems and about the physical aspects of the Trek, given my various health problems, God had taken away.

Yes the trek itself was not without great difficulties for me and it was a huge physical and emotional challenge but I made it, in my own time, at my own pace and more surprisingly, (why should I be surprised?), without any aches or pains, blisters, sore feet, altitude sickness, injuries etc.

If this was not God looking after me, I don't know what was He even surrounded me with guardian angels. The ever reliable, kind, Dandi, the patient and encouraging Dawa, 'The Doc', the willing and helpful guides and porters and, of course, my new found friends of our trekking group who never complained about having to wait for me and all of whom were greatly encouraging and supportive of me. I could not have wished for a better group of people to share this huge, immensely challenging adventure with me. I was, indeed, truly blessed.

I must, of course, not forget those back home who, in their own way, were also on the journey with me. My wife, Elizabeth, who initially really didn't want me to go but, once I had made the decision gave me all the help and encouragement I needed. My children and grandchildren who set up my webpage, blog and the social media funding pages for me and messaged all their friends to tell them about their daft old Dad and which resulted in lots of sponsorship funding.

My friends, both from outside and inside the church fellowship and the prayers of many, many others. I had worried if I would be able to get enough funding to be able to give any meaningful amounts of money to my two charities but once again my worries proved to be groundless and I was hugely blessed by the financial gifts I was given and the donations pledged.

However, this was never solely about money, although both charities will benefit. It was also about promoting the work and Christian ethos of service to others by The Leprosy Mission and the Rainbow of Hope, which I know from my conversations at home and among my fellow travellers here in Nepal, has now become more widely known and appreciated. So, in all ways, Job Done!

17
Return to Kathmandu

My alarm rang at 5.30am. to enable me to get up in time to see the forecasted early morning sunrise over the snow capped Annapurna range of mountains. Other guests must have been told the same thing because many were out with their cameras at the ready. However, we all had our hopes shattered because, although the hotel and gardens were bathed in warm, early morning sunshine, the magnificent panorama of the distant mountain range was shrouded in mist.

I waited for about an hour or so to see if the mist would clear but it didn't and as an added disappointment, it started to rain. There was nothing for it but to return to the hotel for breakfast. It rained heavily for the next two hours, until, finally I managed to get back to my room but there was still no clear view of the mountains. What a disappointment, as this hoped for view and photo opportunity was the main reason that I had decided to stay at this particular hotel, rather than one down at the Phewa lakeside.

'The Boy', the elderly porter, eventually came to carry my bag back down the five hundred steps to the taxi Dawa had ordered for me. Hopefully there will be no more steps for me to encounter on this trip. The taxi arrived on time for the long drive back down the hill and onto Pokhara airport a journey that took nearly two hours but at least I wasn't walking any more. The small airport which had seemed to be full of excited trekkers when I arrived there from Kathmandu, was now very quiet with hardly anyone there at all.

Having checked in my luggage and while sitting

waiting for the plane to arrive, I fell into conversation with a couple from Holland, who, like me, were somewhat older than most of the others undertaking treks. While we were comparing stories of the problems that older trekkers faced, they asked me what I was doing there on my own. I was pleased to tell them my reasons for being there and the lady became very interested to learn about the work of The Leprosy Mission. Like many others I have met, she had no idea that leprosy, in her words, "still existed". Once again God was presenting me with an opportunity to witness about TLM's Christian ethos and my own Faith.

Finally, our plane took off on my return flight to Kathmandu where Dawa was waiting for me to take me back to the Hotel Tibet International where I was to spend my final night. As he was not going to pick me up until late afternoon the next day, he arranged for my check out time to be extended so that I would have the benefit of my hotel room rather than to spend my time waiting in the foyer.

Once settled in my room, I indulged myself in all its modern facilities and took a long hot shower before relaxing in a hot soapy bath, something I haven't done in years, trying to justify my actions by telling myself that it was good for all my aches and pains. This was obviously not true because, although there were times when I was so thoroughly exhausted that I felt that I could not carry on, not once in all my training and on the Trek itself, did I suffer from any aches or pains. My arthritic knees didn't bother me, except walking downhill, nor did I suffer from blisters nor aching feet although I must admit to having cramps in my legs on occasions while sleeping.

God had quite clearly honoured my attempts, in His Name. He had given me the strength to complete the Trek and had kept me safe during all my difficulties on this challenging task.

That evening I went out to explore the very busy streets of Kathmandu and to try to find my way back to the restaurant where we had eaten on the first night but couldn't find it. Furthermore, although I didn't feel apprehensive or nervous, I was conscious that I was on my own, whereas, the last time I was here I was among my trekking companions and being guided by Dawa, so I decided to return to my hotel.

The hotel's 'Shanghai Kitchen', was a fusion of Nepalese, Chinese, Indian and Malay cuisine and I was spoiled for choice and over indulged myself. I started with Narwati chicken Mo Mo's ,(Nepalese steam dumplings) which I had grown to like, accompanied with three different very, very hot dips, much too hot for my taste but the dumplings were lovely. This first course was followed by, 'The Chef's Special', which was one of my favourite rice dishes, Nasi Goreng, delicious but far too much for one person and I have a very healthy appetite! I was much too full for anything else, so declined the offer of desert and coffee and retired to my room.

It was now only 8.30pm, so I settled down to watch an English language news channel, followed by a sports channel showing Manchester United v Sunderland, which somewhat surprisingly Sunderland won 0-1. At the end of the game it showed the results of the other English Premier League matches from which I learnt that Cardiff City had lost to Newcastle United, 3-0 and so were relegated with still two matches to play before the season ended!

So to bed. My last night in Kathmandu. A large, comfortable, double bed but with the same problem of waking every two hours or so before being fully awake at 7.00am.

18
Homeward Bound

My last day in Nepal. Breakfast was taken on the roof terrace in beautiful sunshine. If only it had been like this at the Raniban Retreat to see the wonderful, snow capped, Annapurna Range of the Himalayas. Missing those views that I had hoped to see was only a small disappointment in the whole of my stay in this wonderful country. I had come to see the work of The Leprosy Mission and face the challenge of trekking in the Himalayas and I had done both of those things.

After breakfast I decided to go back to see the Boudhanath Stupa and take in the colourful scenes and the hustle and bustle of the market and shops which surround it. The area was packed with people, with lots going on and tourists of all nationalities mingling with the locals, there was noise and colour everywhere. I found a seat and took some time to take it all in and was interested to see a Nepali lady going around the Stupa, alternatively laying flat out on the floor with her arms stretching out in front of her, then walking a few steps before prostrating herself again and repeating the ritual.

I realised that she was worshipping her gods and it reminded me that it was Sunday so I took some time to carry out my own silent prayers and worship and to send a text message to Richard, the Pastor of my church, to let the fellowship know that I was safe and well and appreciated their prayers of support.

Back at the hotel with still plenty of time left before my extended check out time, I spent some time back on the roof terrace with a large pot of the lovely Nepalese coffee and read an English edition of the previous week's Sunday Times. Eventually I checked out of the hotel but there were still another two hours before I was to be picked up.

Dawa arrived on time and presented me with a medal for successfully completing the Trek and also gave me a beautiful Nepalese prayer shawl. He was gracious enough to say that my slowness on the climbs were of no problem to him and that he had been surprised by my tenacity to complete each day without complaining.

We finally set off through the colourful streets, teaming with people and vehicles, until we arrived at the airport where we said our goodbyes. Once again I was on my own but this time I was heading for home.

After I had checked in and passed through security I was pleased to see the Dutch couple I had met at Pokhara Airport. They welcomed me like an old friend and the lady was eager to tell me that she had looked up the work of The Leprosy Mission and was pleased to learn that TLM had offices in Holland and that she intended to tell all her friends about all the wonderful work that TLM does. I was delighted as although, in undertaking my 'Trek of Hope', I hoped to be able to promote the work of TLM and Rainbow of Hope, I had expected it to be among my friends and neighbours, not internationally. Isn't God wonderful to provide us with different opportunities to witness for Him!

Although we were travelling on the same flight to Abu Dhabi, they were in business class and then flying on to Amsterdam, so once again came the parting of the ways as we boarded different parts of the aircraft. I had booked a window seat for the five hour flight and sat back to relax and to consider all the things that I had experienced since I left home. Then all my memories came flooding back!

My first impressions of the heat, noise, colours and crowds of people in Kathmandu. Seeing the basic condition of the hospital wards at Anandaban. The awful disabilities of the leprosy patients, counter balanced by the new hope they had been given by the surgery and treatment they had received. The Christian faith in action, as shown by the love, dedication and skills of the surgeons, doctors and nurses.

The wonderful smiling faces of the Nepalese people. The first meeting with Dawa and those I would be trekking with, including the faithful Dandi, 'The Doc.' and the other guides, sherpas and porters. The difficulties of each day's climb. The fourteen thousand steps. All the different sights and sounds of the people we met on our way in the remote villages and, of course the majestic scenery of the beautiful Annapurna Range of the mighty Himalayas.

It had been a wonderful experience, much more than I could have hoped for. Underpinned by the loving and prayerful support and encouragement of family and friends back home and, of course, by the Grace of God, who was with me every (thousands!) step of the way. I was and am, truly blessed!

I had a long wait changing flights at Abu Dhabi airport, made worse by there being no seats in the waiting area. After the numerous difficulties I faced on the trek itself having to sit or lie on the floor was but a small problem.

Once on board the aircraft to London, again comfortably in a window seat, I was at last able to completely relax and drifted off into a deep sleep for a couple of hours. It was quite an uneventful flight and, relatively quickly we were safely touching down at Heathrow and through the baggage collection and customs.

Elizabeth and our daughter, Derian, were there to meet me and then followed an emotional reunion with me promising Elizabeth that I would not go anywhere without her ever again! We had a good journey home in the car, with me going on and on about all the many experiences I had encountered on my wonderful adventure and arrived back home to an enthusiastic welcome party from our son-in-law, Richard and our three grandchildren. I really couldn't have asked for anything more!

Many had said, "You must be crazy!" when I announced that I was to undertake my 'Trek of Hope' and there were many times before and during that difficult challenge that I must say that I felt the same way myself but, I made it!

Made it in and through God's grace and in His strength. I had listened to 'His still small voice' and had answered it. As a result, I truly believe that God had honoured my actions and had blessed and supported me, 'every step of the way', during my struggles which served to help fund and to make known the on-going work of, 'The Leprosy Mission, England and Wales' and the 'Rainbow of Hope' and to be a witness to HIS great Love.

Part 3
An Unfinished Story?

1
Further Adventures

I really thought that my adventures and travels had come to an end when I returned home and promised Elizabeth that I would never go anywhere without her ever again. How wrong I was on both counts. It seems that God was not finished with me yet!

So, as a postscript to the story of my 'Trek of Hope' (at least for now), please allow me to update you on a few things that you have already read about and new things that have happened during the five years since my return.

Firstly, you might like to know that in the first year, people, like yourself perhaps, have kindly and very generously, donated £10,000 to my 'Trek of Hope'. The total amount has been divided equally between my two Charities, The Leprosy Mission, England and Wales, and the Rainbow of Hope, working with the homeless and disadvantaged in Cardiff, for their on-going work among those they serve. The money in both small and larger amounts, has been given by hundreds of caring people and also from the proceeds of a 'Thanksgiving Concert', by the World Famous, Treorchy Male Choir which was well received by an appreciative audience of 350, at my home Church, Albany Road Baptist, Cardiff in November 2014.

It was wonderful to see the Church full and the Choir, conducted by it's Musical Director, Jeffery

Howard, who also played the piano and organ in duets with his Wife Rachael, (on the Welsh harp), generously gave their services and talents, free of charge. Since that evening, the Choir has used the Church on four other occasions as it's preferred venue in support of other charitable causes so, as well as making known the work of The Leprosy Mission and Rainbow of Hope, other charities have benefited from and been blessed by these delightful evenings of songs and praise.

On my return home and being asked about my adventures, there seemed to be a genuine interest in why I had undertaken such a challenge. I found this amusing as it was a far cry from the 'You must be crazy!' comments I had received prior to my Trek. A number of organisations from within the Church asked me to speak at their meetings, which I was more than happy to do as they had supported and encouraged me both financially and prayerfully. These evenings were well received and soon word got around and I found myself being asked to speak at other churches and organisations who kindly give me donations towards my 'Trek of Hope' funds.

It was also suggested that my story might be of interest to a local, free, advertising magazine which I approached, somewhat reluctantly and to my surprise my article was accepted. Since then, I have continued to write for the magazine, about the work of TLM and Rainbow of Hope and a number of other local Christian organisations as well as telling about what our Church is doing to reach out to our local community. To my delight, these articles have not been edited in any way and have been generally well accepted. I feel that God is using my experience and new found talents to further

His work.

He, has also given me the strength and courage to take on new ventures, in His name, which I will tell you about next.

2
'Rainbow of Hope'

The 'Rainbow of Hope', is a Cardiff Charity supporting the homeless and disadvantaged in the Capital City of Wales. Teams of between three to six people from different denominations of local churches in Cardiff and the South Wales Valleys go out into the City's street, each night of the year in all weathers providing hot food, sandwiches, hot drinks, sleeping bags and clothing. It also provides food parcels to many in need, single parents, refugees and asylum seekers in the local community. It receives no funding from official bodies and exists solely on donations, mostly food and clothing, through the generosity of the public.

For the last 20 years I have been a member of one of those teams working within a group from my own Church and two other churches and a close bond has been formed through our willingness to serve the less fortunate in our community in any way we can. Generally it has been a worthwhile, humbling and yet rewarding time with our 'clients' being very appreciative of our support. We do it out of a Christian ethos of service but it is given to all in need regardless of no faith or other faiths, indeed, all are welcome. We do not preach; we do not judge; but we are more than willing to be a source of comfort by listening to their problems, especially if asked to pray with or for someone.

Recently, within our small group, we felt that God was challenging us to do something different, as individuals and as a team. We all have busy family and working lives and we were struggling trying to do the all things we needed or wanted to do and at the same time, trying to discern what God wanted us to do next. Having given it prayerful consideration we decided that we would withdraw from our duties at the time of our last 'shift' at the end of December 2017. That evening was particularly difficult as we said our farewells to each other and to the many homeless folk we had come to know as more than just faces or hands reaching out for much needed food, clothing and hope. However, despite missing being out on the streets, we finished safe in the knowledge that through His Grace, God had already reached out to others who were to take our place so that the continuity of service would be maintained.

Three of our group work within our National Health Service and as well as dealing with the daily pressures of their stressful jobs they felt that they we being called to do other work; one with young people; another to help out with church choirs and music groups and the third to be there for elderly parents. My own calling seemed to be for a different kind work within the 'Rainbow of Hope'. I had recently been asked to be one of its Trustees as it seeks to expand its work towards having a permanent place of its own. For the last four years it has been renting a property on a short term tenancy to use as a 'drop in' centre from which it can provide a shop selling (or giving away) clothing and small items of furniture, providing hot meals and hold bible classes and prayer meetings for those who want them and also to give advice for those who may require information on legal matters especially about tenancies or immigration matters The landlord has now put the property up for sale and we are praying that somehow we will be able to purchase it Through knowing of my work with ‘Rainbow of Hope’, a number of folk from our Church Fellowship have wanted to help but felt unable to go out onto the streets, especially at night, so have now become part of the team of volunteers helping in the shop. Through their good work a number of those who visit the shop have started to come to church and over the last year, five have given their lives to God and publicly declared their Faith by going though the waters of baptism at special services in the shop itself. Thanks be to God for providing willing workers to reap His harvest.

3
A New Challenge

For some years I had been asked to become a 'Local Volunteer Speaker', which would mean me visiting Churches and Chapels throughout South Wales to speak about the work of The Leprosy Mission and encouraging individuals and groups to support TLM through prayer and financially.

This I had always resisted as I didn't think that it was something I could do, especially if it meant preaching at Sunday services. Then, together with many other TLM supporters, I received an invitation to attend an area conference in a church in Mumbles, Swansea, which I accepted. Little did I know what lay ahead of me. On arriving at the church, TLM's Area Co-ordinator for Wales, Trevor Grant, asked I would be prepared to tell the meeting about my Trek and why I had decided to do it.

I was taken aback, as I hadn't expected to be asked to do that and was reluctant to face a group of expectant people without having anything prepared. However, having been put on the spot, I felt that there was little to do except to say OK and spend the time before the meeting, recalling my adventures in my head and to earnestly pray for clarity of mind. Once again God did not let me down You would have thought that by now I should have expected that, He allowed me to stand in front of all those people at the Meeting and deliver everything that He laid upon my heart.

My experiences came to life and poured out of my mouth with such feeling and excitement that I had to be asked to come to a finish because I had overrun my allotted time.

My small part of the meeting was well received and afterwards I received many comments of appreciation for undertaking the Trek and promoting awareness of the effect of leprosy in this modern world. I was greatly encouraged by the whole experience and arrived back home that afternoon, thanking God for enabling to speak publicly.

I decided I would accept the request to become a Local Volunteer Speaker for TLM. After sharing this decision with Elizabeth and having her agree that this was the right thing to do, I contacted Trevor Grant to say that I was willing to become part of his area team.

Trevor soon arranged speaking engagements for me and after accompanying me on my first meeting, then felt able to allow me to 'fly solo' so to speak. Since then I have carried out (and I am continuing to do so) many of these meetings to churches and chapels throughout the South Wales region and also at secular organisations such as Rotary Clubs, the 'University of the Third Age' (U3A), Local Government retirement groups and other similar groups.

While they are usually well aware of the extent of the problem of the homeless, they know little or nothing about the effect of leprosy in the poorer counties throughout the world. Although I am an unpaid volunteer, at these meetings the organisations and groups I speak to are very generous in the speakers fee and individual donations given to me and as well as, in the case of the churches and chapels, becoming partners in prayer and at the same time they are being made aware of the on-going work of the two Charities.

4
Disaster!

On the 25 April 2015, almost exactly twelve months after my return from Nepal, the country was hit by a huge earthquake which registered at 7.8 on the Richter scale quickly followed by two after shocks of magnitudes 6.6 and 6.7. Massive damage was done to large areas of Nepal and over 9000 people were killed, 2,500 of them children. To compound the disaster on the 12 May, another after shock with a magnitude of 7.3 occurred just north of Kathmandu which resulted in another 100 people being killed with many more injured.

The television coverage of the devastation to the Capital City, Kathmandu, was graphic and showed the substantial damage to homes and offices but the full story of the effect of the earthquake could not be shown. Major damage was done to the many remote villages that are scattered about the Himalayas and because of their remoteness from the transportation system, many of these villages are only accessible on foot and the camera crews could not reach them. Many have been totally destroyed, including perhaps, some of those I may have stayed in while on my Trek and as well as lives being lost, so too have gone their homes and animals upon which they depend for their food and livelihoods.

Despite parts of its hospital being hit by the earthquake the doctors, nurses and other medical staff of The Leprosy Mission at Anandaban went out with the rescue services to search among these villages for survivors and provide such medical assistance and comforting help as may be necessary.

The whole area continued to be affected by after shocks and it was considered to be unsafe to live and work within buildings so much of the medical work had to be carried out in tents used as makeshift operating theatres and hospital wards. The staff were fully occupied for many months caring, not only for their regular leprosy patients but also large numbers of the local people needing medical treatment for their injuries as a result of the earthquake.

Knowing the difficulties they faced and remembering many of the staff and others I had met on my Trek I was naturally concerned and was frustrated by how little I could do as it had been decreed that only qualified and experienced medical and rescue teams should attempt to go to the region to help. There was little I could do from a distance except cover in prayer the whole of Nepal and especially those with TLM and others working with Christian aid organisations and to try to raise funds for the rebuilding of the hospital at Anandaban and its clinic in Patan, Kathmandu and this I set out to do. Then, the following year an answer to my prayers came out of the blue, which was to give me another opportunity to revisit Nepal.

Trevor Grant was to lead a group of Local Volunteer Speakers on a visit to India in October 2016 and I was asked if I wished to go. Yes, of course I would but I had promised Elizabeth that I wouldn't go anywhere without her again.

When she heard about this opportunity her immediate response was, "Yes of course you should go. It will give you more experiences that will help you to speak at your meetings!" and she added, "At the end of the trip you could ‘pop over’ to Nepal and revisit the hospital at Anandaban!”

What another God given opportunity for me to increase my knowledge of the work of TLM in India and to see for myself how my friends in Anandaban were coping as well as being able to meet up with my old friend Dawa, the Chief Sherpa on my ‘Trek of Hope’, to thank him for looking after me so well.

5
Return to India

Once again problems arose for my visit to India and subsequently Nepal. Again I came up against the reluctance of the airlines to allow me to fly on to Nepal if I was booked in a party. So, once again, I had to book my own flights.

This I was able to do and to their credit the airline, Jet Airways, allowed me to book on the same flight from London Heath Row to Kolkata (formerly Calcutta) with our group and at the end of my time with them, to fly onwards to Kathmandu for my stay in Nepal and afterwards home to the UK from Kathmandu, via Delhi.

After arriving at Heath Row to meet up with Trevor and his wife, Liz, I was introduced to the rest of my fellow travellers. There were twelve of us (there's that reassuring number again!), like me, Local Volunteer Speakers, not all from Wales, just two of us this time but others from different regions of the UK. We quickly settled on our plane and we were off. As I had booked independently, I was not seated with our group so did not get a chance to speak with them until we arrived at our hotel in Delhi but over supper that evening we caught up before we went to our rooms early as it had been a long day and we were getting up at 5.00am to catch an early train for a six hour journey to the little township of Purulia where we were to visit The Leprosy Mission hospital.

We were supposed to leave early but as we were to learn, everything in India is late, except their brilliant train service. When our bus arrived, nearly an hour late, we were driven as fast as the driver could through the colourful, noisy, diverse city that is Kolkata. Even at that early hour the railway station was a seething mass of humanity all rushing to different platforms to catch their trains to destinations all over India. After fighting our way through the crowds and hauling our suitcases over a series of high footbridges to the furthest platform of the station we were horrified to see our train slowly beginning to move off. Knowing India's pride for the punctuality of its train services we were resigned to miss our train, the only one to be heading to our remote destination that week. Someone must have uttered a quick prayer of desperation for, as if by a miracle, the train suddenly stopped and we thankfully clambered on.

Once settled in our reserved seats we began to relax and excitedly shared our thoughts about what we would have done if we had missed the train. All was well until I realised that I had lost my new mobile phone, acquired especially for this trip. It had either fallen out of my pocket in the crazy scramble at the station or I had become victim to, reputedly, the world's best pick pockets. If so, they are very good indeed, I didn't feel a thing. My relaxed demeanour suddenly became something akin to the swans on the lake of my local park, all calm and serene on the surface and a mass of panic underneath. What could I to do without my phone? I am generally not one who needs my phone constantly but this time I was worried about losing all my personal data, phone numbers, flight details etc. There was nothing that I could do about it other than inform my service provider to cancel or stop my contract so that I wouldn't face possible huge bills by others using it. Yet despite me advising them, two months after I arrived home I found that a large amount had been debited from my account. Upon checking it was found that the same day that I had 'lost' my phone, someone had used it to purchase a lap top computer which had been delivered to an address in London, UK. Luckily my provider and bank believed my version of events and my 'debt' was cancelled.

6
Purulia Hospital

Our six hour train and bus journey to Purulia Hospital completed, we received a warm welcome and were taken to the Guest House where we were to spend the next four days. I was to share a room with Dave and soon settled into the rather sparse and basic bedroom before taking a cold shower to refresh myself after our early start to the day and the long, hot train journey. The shower was refreshing, with a strong jet of cold water shooting out of the wall through a hole where the shower head had once been. The bathroom itself was very basic too, consisting of concrete floor and walls, no tiles and a small washbasin and toilet in the opposite corner to the shower. Supper over, we all chatted for a while before bed and hoping for a good night's rest before another early start.

The next morning we joined with doctors, nurses and some patients for the customary morning service in the large church set in the hospital grounds. Following the service we visited the hospital and after being given a short history of the work being carried out we were invited to visit the wards. They were similar to those I had seen on my previous visits to India and Nepal but came as a shock to most of the others in our party. Basic but very functional and acceptable to the patients, the old, metal, military style beds, bedding and lighting left a lot to be desired and came as a great surprise to those more used to hospitals in the UK. What couldn't be faulted was the treatment and nursing the patients received, nor the loving care, professionalism and commitment of all the staff.

Vocational Training Centre, tailoring class

The operating theatres too were pretty basic but not so the skills of the surgeons, doctors and nurses which were on a par to our own medical teams. We were allowed to observe operations to correct clawed hands, dropped feet, ulcerated legs and eye operations all associated with the affect of leprosy and it was a great privilege to see, at close quarters, such skilled surgeons at work. These were general surgical operations, following which, after a period of rehabilitation, the patients soon recovered and allowed to return home. However our visit to the wards housing those with ulcerated legs and feet was harrowing. Leprosy effects the nerve endings at the extremity of the body and hands and feet and they become vulnerable to cuts and burns. If not treated immediately, the wounds become infected, ulcers form and begin to eat away at the flesh and the bones resulting, more often than not, in amputation of the affected parts and the subsequent need for artificial limbs which are tailor made for the patients by The Leprosy Mission's craftsmen on site.

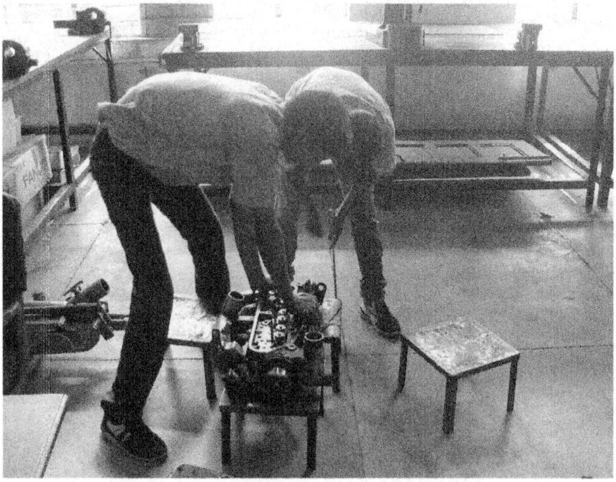

Vocational Training Centre, engineering class

The following morning we visited The Leprosy Mission's Colony on the outskirts of Purulia. We were greeted with smiles and warmth by the residents of this remote colony who seemed pleased that people from the other side of the world had come to visit them and show interest in their lives and in themselves. Nearly all the residents were elderly, with severe deformities from the effects of leprosy and we were welcomed into their homes, small two room dwellings, with no running water, gas nor electricity but each of the residents beamed with the pride of ownership of their own individual space. There were communal wash rooms and toilets and small individual gardens, vegetable plots and even chicken runs to provide meat and eggs.

Isolated but happy with wonderful smiling faces which masked their physical deformities, they were a joy to be with and to share their world, if only for a short few hours.

Our visit was a wonderful, humbling experience that I shall never forget, especially one incident that brought me to tears. While we were waiting for our transport back to the guest house I sat down on the steps of one of the homes.

Leprosy Colony, Kathmandu. An elderly resident

Silently, without warning, out of the deep darkness of the shade, an elderly lady, moving only on her bottom, slid up to me and laid her head on my shoulder, smiling broadly she held my hand and whispered, "Thank you." I was unable to do anything but put a protective arm around her shoulder, give her a hug and whisper back, "Nameste. Thank you and may God bless you," before we had to leave.

Leprosy Colony, Purulia. Lady out of the shadows.

Our last day at Purulia was spent at TLM's Educational and Vocational Centre where young men and women, some with leprosy and others whose mothers or fathers have leprosy, have an opportunity to spend a year being taught dress making and tailoring, car mechanics, welding, information technology and administration skills. They sit nationally recognised examinations and if successful are awarded qualifications which become their pathway to self worth through being accepted by local and national employers and which enables them to provide an income for their families. Some are also able to set up their own businesses and we visited one young man who had done exactly that and he now employs seven others in his flourishing motor bike garage. Through these wonderful training centres much hope is given to leprosy sufferers to live a fulfilling life and to sustain their families.

Our time at Purulia over, we said our farewells

and were soon back on the train heading back to Kolkata where we spent another night before flying on to Delhi for the 'holiday' part of our trip. A day's sightseeing and shopping before getting up early the next day for a four hour bus ride to Agra to see the world famous Taj Mahal (beautiful) and Agra Fort (magnificent). There was only one problem, it was the last day of the Hindu Diwali 'Festival of Lights' and getting out of Agra was almost impossible. The streets were crowed with happy revellers and all the traffic was completely grid locked. Two hours of getting nowhere then, as if on a given signal, the traffic started moving and we were on our way back to Delhi. The anticipated four hour journey took more than six hours to get back to our hotel.

No time nor inclination for supper. Straight to bed for another early morning start for the airport.

7
Return to Nepal

The airport at Delhi was a parting of the ways for me from my travelling companions. They were flying home and I was off to Kathmandu. Why? you may ask. Well you may remember that when Elizabeth said that I should go on this trip to India, she also voiced the thought that I should, "Pop over to Nepal to revisit the TLM hospital at Anandaban." It made sense that as I was so close. I could see at first hand the damage that was done by the earthquakes in 2015, so that was what I was going to do. Once again I was greeted at the airport by the familiar truck driver who skilfully but very slowly worked his way through the busy streets. Kathmandu was still in the process of recovery, most if not all the collapsed or damaged buildings had been cleared away but the roads were still in a very bad state and the pollution from rotting food and animal carcases and the dust that covers everything and everyone is all embracing. Once out of the City and climbing up into the mountains, while the roads were in a poor state and buildings damaged, thankfully the air was much clearer.

On reaching the hospital I could see the extent of the damage. The doctors and nurses quarters had been demolished and other parts of the hospital, including one of the wards had been damaged and had to be repaired Even the substantial brick built guest house I had stayed in on my last visit had not escaped the earthquake and had to be demolished. All that was left of it was now just a cleared site.

I was told, that at the time of the earthquake and the numerous aftershocks it was deemed prudent to move out from buildings and the work of operations and aftercare treatment were carried out in a number of large tents, hastily erected on what little flat ground as was available on the steeply sloping site. While this arrangement was not very satisfactory, the usual high standard of the treatment and care for the patients was maintained, as was the additional work with the injured from the local population as a result of the earthquake.

Elizabeth and I with Shovakar, TLM Hospital administrator

The next morning I was taken to Patan on the outskirts of Kathmandu to see the brand new outpatients clinic. Like many of the buildings in Kathmandu the old clinic had been badly damaged and was now, 'not fit for purpose'. After much prayer and a comprehensive search a suitable building had been found and purchased by TLM. It was close to the old clinic and provided all the facilities needed to carry out all the services required for the purpose.

I had expressed a wish to visit the local leprosy

colony and that afternoon I was taken on an hour long drive out of Kathmandu to the TLM colony village. My guide for the afternoon was a young nurse from Anandaban, who as a child, had lived in the village with her parents, both of whom were leprosy sufferers. She and I were made most welcome, especially by those who remembered her living amongst them. Nearly two hundred people live there in fairly modern, small, yet comfortable, one or two bedroom dwellings which house individuals, couples and families who suffer from leprosy. The atmosphere was lovely and I was invited into their homes by the proud occupants to be offered cold drinks and small items of food. As with the leprosy colony I had visited in India, the accommodation was very basic, with no running water nor gas, however, a small amount of electricity was generated by small solar panels which had been generously provided by a British company. I was left with the general impression that all those in the colony were very happy to be living there in a loving, supportive community, despite having to cope with their disabilities.

Leaving the community, we realised that we had stayed too long and would probably miss our evening meal by the time we arrived back at the hospital so we decided to eat in Kathmandu. This turned out to be quite an experience as I was taken into one of the many Mo Mo eating houses in the City. I had said that I loved Mo Mo's, a kind of steamed dumpling filled with minced chicken or vegetables but these were quite unlike those served in more modern establishments. The small single room was crowded with young people which made the room, already full of steam from the cooking, very hot indeed. Not as hot though as the large, spicy Mo Mo's themselves and the accompanying dips that come with them. Washed down with cold drinks, they were delicious. I was the only European there and was accepted with much friendliness and in turn, seemed to provide my fellow diners with much hilarity from my discomfort of these spicy treats.

Events like this must be experienced to be enjoyed and will long live in my memory, as will the good humour and delightful smiles of the residents of the leprosy colony and the sterling work of all the staff at the hospital.

8
A Sherpa in Kathmandu

My time in Nepal was all too short but I did bring a Sherpa home with me! More of that below. Having said my farewells to the staff at Anandaban Hospital, I was driven from the peace and serenity of the mountains back into the chaos that is Kathmandu, to my oasis of calm, the Hotel Tibet International where I soon enjoyed the luxury of a warm shower and fresh, clean clothes.

I had arranged to meet up with Dawa, the Chief Sherpa on my 'Trek of Hope', two years previously. We enjoyed a lovely meal together and while reminiscing about our trekking adventure, I was amazed and delighted to learn that he was travelling to Wales the next day but unfortunately not on the same flight, to visit a primary school in Bridgend which supported the aims and vision of his charity. During his visit to Wales, it was my pleasure to meet up with him and share time together.

He told me of the difficulties of the children living in the remote villages in the high Himalayas. There were very few schools and those children who were lucky enough to live near to their local school often faced a daily round trip of up to three to four hours walk, over steep rough dirt tracks, often in very bad weather, to get to the few state run infants and junior schools in the area. Many children are unable to complete their education because they are required to work on their family's land or find some other means of earning money to support their families. Those fortunate enough to go on to secondary education often had to leave their homes to go to the larger towns and cities where these schools were situated and many of them decide to not return home at the end of their schooling. The combined effect of these actions is to weaken their communities and threaten the traditions and a way of life that has existed for centuries, Dawa himself, at the age of 11 ran away from his home of Lukla, near the base of Mount Everest to go to Kathmandu to further his education and this experience made him determined to help ease the problem for other children. Now, many years later he has founded a charity called 'Classrooms in the Clouds', an organisation supported by donations from individuals and companies throughout the world, to build small schools in some of the remotest villages. These schools cater for mixed age range of between 5 and 15 and would be staffed in the early stages by experienced volunteer teachers from the UK and other Countries working alongside trainee Nepalese teachers.

The Charity, also known by its acronym, CITC, is now a registered Non-Governmental Organisation (NGO) in Nepal and a Registered Charity in the UK. Both are staffed entirely by volunteers and had originally intended to build just two classrooms in Dawa's home village of Lukla but with the success of that project it has steadily grown in confidence which has enabled it to extend the work. It has developed a rolling three year plan of selecting appropriate sites, design work, raise the necessary funds and build. It now has built over forty classrooms or schools at five locations, each with gender specific toilets and hygiene facilities, libraries and IT suites. It employs two local Nepalese, one as an Education Development Manager and the other as an Education Support Worker. Particular emphasis is given to support women in education. Eight out of their ten sponsored teachers are women who provide excellent role models for young girls in country areas where education for girls is limited and as a means of addressing some of the barriers that exist which prevents them from completing their education.

Young girl from leprosy colony whose future education is being sponsored by TLM Australia

This worthy venture, as well as providing education for the children and young people, has the added benefit of developing different skills to the older generation, such as, teaching, administration and management work, as well as building skills for the local men. It also encourages ownership and sustainability over the longer term. In many ways CITC's ideals are very similar to the work of the two Charities, I support, The Leprosy mission and Rainbow of Hope, in its service to and working with, those most in need and I am proud to be able support my good friend Dawa in his vision to help educate the children of Nepal's remote mountain villages.

My flight home gave me time to reflect on my new experiences with TLM in India and my subsequent short visit to Nepal to see how the 2015 earthquake had affected the hospital. To be able to meet up again with Dawa and learn how his 'Classrooms in the Clouds' is helping the children of the remote villages in the Himalayas has been inspiring, rewarding and informative.

I am humbled by what others are doing to serve the less fortunate in their communities with little or no help from the authorities and simply relying on donations, often sacrificially, given from their many supporters throughout the world. and I thank God for His provision to meet these needs.

In some ways this trip had been (almost) as difficult as my 'Trek of Hope'. Not quite as physically demanding, although there were times when I struggled in the intense heat, but more harrowing, in seeing some of the more serious outcomes of the effect of leprosy on different parts of the body and its life changing consequences. Also seeing the devastation that earthquakes can cause in so many lives, especially in the remote mountain communities, which in some instances have been completely destroyed. I am now, more than ever, filled with the need to help in any way I can from my geographical distance and more importantly, covering both India and Nepal in prayer.

9
Yet another return to India and Nepal

Well, I never thought that it would happen but I have been fortunate to go back again but this time on a holiday.

Early in 2018, 'out of the blue', so to speak, in the middle of my e-mails, up popped a travel agents advertisement promoting a twelve day holiday to Nepal and India at almost half the usual price. I thought that this would be a great opportunity to take my Wife to show her the Nepal and India that I have grown to love. Elizabeth has never felt the need to come with me on my travels, especially as she doesn't like the heat and the idea of having to use the basic accommodation and facilities I had encountered on my previous visits didn't appeal to her either. I thought that it was an opportunity too good to lose so persisted in trying to get her to say yes.

It took all my persuasive powers to get her to agree. I argued that this was going to be a holiday, not a trek nor an investigative visit to see the work of TLM at first hand, despite her interest and constant support of me and TLM. In the end she succumbed, not entirely due to my persuasion but to the fact that we would be staying in 4/5 star hotels with swimming pools and en-suite bathrooms and travelling in air conditioned buses. Plus and this was the big deal breaker, the chance, while in Nepal, to visit The Leprosy Mission hospital at Anandaban, which she had heard so much about. There was also in India, a scheduled visit to the beautiful Taj Mahal, where I promised, (somewhat jokingly) I would take her photograph on the same bench that the late,

Diana, Princess of Wales, had her picture taken, which was circulated throughout the world.

Having had her agreement I quickly booked the holiday before she changed her mind. There could be no backing out now.

The big day eventually arrived and we travelled to Heathrow to catch our ten hour flight, via Delhi, to Kathmandu. The long flight was comfortable and uneventful and on our arrival in Nepal we were driven through the now familiar (to me), colourful, crowded, noisy streets to our overnight hotel, the Hotel Tibet. Then came my first disappointment. It was not the familiar Hotel Tibet International at which I had stayed on my previous visits but a smaller sister hotel of the same franchise but nevertheless comfortable and a good standard for Nepal. My disappointment was that I had expected that we would be staying at my usual hotel and had arranged to meet Dawa there the following evening and we were now staying in a different location on the other side of the city.

On our first evening our tour manager had arranged for us to eat out at a nearby Nepalese restaurant where we enjoyed several varieties of the local food and were entertained by a traditional dance group. We arrived back at our hotel very tired after almost twenty four hours of travelling and looking forward to a good night's sleep before setting out for the hospital the following morning.

The day had been scheduled as a sightseeing tour of Kathmandu but we opted out and instead had arranged to visit The Leprosy Mission Hospital at Anandaban, some fifteen miles north of Kathmandu.

10
Back at Anandaban

After breakfast we were picked up our hotel by Dr, Shovakhar Kandel, The Leprosy Mission's Regional Manager in Nepal who warmly welcomed me back. I was pleased that he recognised me from my previous visit and he, in turn, was pleased that this time I had brought Elizabeth with me.

We drove the relatively short distance to the new out patients clinic at Patan just in time to join the staff at their morning prayers which was deeply moving, before being proudly shown around the modern and well equipped premises. You may remember that earlier I mentioned that much prayer had gone into considering the purchase of a suitable premises for a new clinic, well those prayers had been fully answered and blessed. Shovakhar told us that, surprisingly, while TLM Nepal had to purchase the land on which it stood, the owner included at no extra charge, the whole building. Another wonderful example of the power of prayer! Then we were off again through the City and out along the still badly earthquake damaged roads and soon we were climbing up into the fresh, clear air of the mountains to Anandaban, which rather beautifully translates as, 'The Forest of Joy'. A very appropriate name for such a lovely area and for the joy the hospital residents feel from the loving support and healing they receive.

At the hospital we were greeted like old friends and this was quite overwhelming for Elizabeth as to visit the hospital was the main reason that she had agreed to come on this holiday to see for herself the wonderful work that I have been speaking about since my first visit. A new 'Guest House' is in the process of being built to replace the old one which was badly damaged by the earthquake and had to be demolished. We were then shown around the old and the newly built wards and met many of the patients and staff.

The rather full morning was rounded off by having lunch (curry, what else?) in the hospital dining room where another surprise awaited us. We suddenly heard another Welsh accent! Among a group of about ten young doctors and nurses, was a lady from Aberdare which is only about twelve miles over the Rhigos mountain from Elizabeth's family home at the top of the Rhondda Valley. It really is a small world, isn't it?

The young lady, Jess, was delighted to meet us and to catch up with news from home. She was training to become a doctor and she and other trainee nurses and doctors from different countries in Europe were in Nepal experiencing the expert orthopaedic medical work that Anandaban provides.

That afternoon we visited TLM's leprosy colony/village which I had seen on my previous visit and which Elizabeth had specifically asked to see. Once again we were invited into the comparatively modern but small homes that the leprosy suffers and their families live in. Of the two hundred residents there a number have children some of whom are leprosy free and attend local schools. We were introduced to one family who proudly told us that their youngest daughter had been awarded a scholarship, funded by The Leprosy Mission of Australia, which will provide her with all her educational costs and fees right through to leaving university. A huge opportunity for her, especially in a country where girls often have their education cut short by family demands or early marriages.

Our day ended with us meeting up with Dawa for supper at the Hotel Tibet International. We did not eat at the hotel, instead Dawa took us on a short walking tour to see the area around Boudhanath Stupa, the largest temple in Nepal and a national heritage site. The busy streets were full of local people and tourists visiting the Stupa and the multitude of shops and restaurants in the surrounding square. We ate at a rooftop restaurant where we once again enjoyed delicious Mo Mo's as well as other local specialities, while enjoying the colourful scene in the streets below.

From our high vantage point we were able to see the roof of the Stupa which, unfortunately had been badly damaged by the affects of the 2015 earthquake and the extent of the work being carried out to repair it.

Our meal over we said our farewell to Dawa and returned to our hotel tired after another full day. We, especially Elizabeth, had thoroughly enjoyed our time TLM's hospital and leprosy village where we were inspired by the work being carried out to help those with leprosy and their families.

11
Sightseeing and Soaring Temperatures

After a good night's sleep we enjoyed a substantial breakfast before meeting our two fellow tourists, Paul and Honoria from London, and boarded our mini bus to continue our holiday of Nepal and India. Leaving Kathmandu we had an eight hour journey to Pokhara, the gateway to the Himalayas. We were to stay for the next two nights at the shoreline of the beautiful Lake Fewa, a lovely holiday destination although we couldn't tell that evening as we arrived in pouring rain and a spectacular electrical storm.

What a welcome! I had forgotten how it rains in Nepal. The next morning we woke to a completely different day. A cloudless, beautiful blue sky and brilliant sunshine that sent the temperature soaring into the high 30 degrees. We were looking forward to the scheduled boat trip on the lake, expecting a pleasant journey on a sturdy launch, complete with comfortable seating where we could sit and sip cold drinks while admiring the lovely scenery. Yes, there were a lot of lovely sights but our craft turned out to be nothing more than a flimsy, four person canoe which we perilously squashed into while our oarsman calmly sat high on the stern expertly guiding us on an hour long trip around the lake.

Safely off the boat we spent the afternoon sightseeing around Pokhara which was very interesting except that we wilted under the oppressive heat and humidity and asked to be taken back early to our hotel so that we could cool off in the swimming pool. Unfortunately our time in the pool was cut short by yet another of Nepal's electrical storms which had us quickly running to the safety of our rooms.

The next day, a hot, sticky, five hour journey to our next stop, Nagarkot, was over increasingly rough roads until we reached the outskirts of the town. Then another hour's climb up and along a steep dangerous mountain road that was little more than a track, to the grandeur of our hotel, situated at the very top of a mountain, which had the most spectacular views over the valley far below. A beautiful but isolated hotel with no swimming pool and nothing to do except to go walking which, due to the steepness of the terrain and the stifling heat, was not really an option for us.

All we could do the following day was to have a leisurely breakfast and relax with our books and spent the rest of the time until supper by packing our bags ready for the morning. If this hotel stop was to give us time to relax after all our travelling, it was perfect.

That night we went to bed early trying not to think to much about the prospect of the trip back down the steep mountain track. As it turned out , while it had its hair raising moments especially when passing other vehicles, it was not as bad as we feared and soon we were back at Kathmandu airport for our flight to India and the next step of our holiday.

The two hour flight to Delhi hardly gave us just enough time to settle into our seats before we were once again in the usual rush to get off the plane, grab our luggage off the carousel and go through immigration and passport controls before we were once again out into the fresh air. I say fresh air but it was a wall of forty six degree heat that hit us. Nepal had been hot but this was something else. No cool mountain breeze, just heat. I have never encountered anything like it on my previous visits and worried about Elizabeth. Thankfully we were soon into our air conditioned mini bus and on our way to Agra, some one hundred and forty miles away and five hours later we arrived at our hotel completely exhausted.

We had stayed in lovely hotels in Nepal but this was five star luxury, with beautiful bedrooms, comfortable beds and an open air swimming pool on the roof. The night air was still very warm and the pool refreshingly cool but our swim was not without its problems. While our two travelling companions and I were able to get into the water easily, Elizabeth had more of a problem because the metal hand rails were still too hot to hold and the metal steps into the water were not flat but tubular which made them painful to stand on. Eventually Elizabeth lowered herself into the water and really enjoyed her swim.

However getting out of the pool proved to be more of a problem for her than getting in had been. Once again she couldn't hold the still hot hand rails and the tubular design of the steeps meant that she was in pain standing on them.

Then followed several minutes of almost slapstick comedy which we are sorry that nobody filmed as it would be a joy to see again during the dreary nights of a British winter.

With our two friends trying to pull Elizabeth out and me, nearly drowning under water with my head under her 'derrière', so that she wouldn't slip back into the water, she eventually flopped out onto the side of the pool, where, in her own words, she lay, "like a beached whale!"

The problem was compounded by the fact that she has a replacement (metal) knee and is not allowed to kneel on it, which made it very difficult for her to get out of the pool.

However, the difficulties were soon forgotten as we were able to sit outside in the balmy night, under a star filled sky, drinking hot coffee (beer for the men) and having a good laugh about it. Yet another incident to tuck away in our memory scrapbook of this wonderful trip, which you might remember, was one that Elizabeth had to be persuaded to take.

One of her conditions was that we would visit the leprosy hospital (tick) and colony (tick), to be able to stay in comfortable hotels (tick) and to visit the Taj Mahal, which is next on our itinerary, so roll on tomorrow.

12
The Taj Mahal

Today was the third event that Elizabeth put on her 'wish list' when she decided to come on this adventure with me, our visit to the Taj Mahal, and a must see attraction for all those who are fortunate to come to this part of India. Just a short drive to the site through the already packed streets full of people of all nationalities, who like us, had come to see this 'Wonder of the World'. Having passed through the long security queues we made our climb up to the main entrance, a perfect portal which framed our first sight of the iconic building we had all come to see.

Even from that distance, the building made familiar by countless thousands of photographs that nearly everyone has seen, was wonderful. Its stunning silhouette has that 'Wow!' factor. Although it was my third visit it still took my breath away and Elizabeth and our travelling companions just stared in silent wonder. It really does have that effect on those seeing it for the first time.

The Taj Mahal is not a mosque, nor a temple. It is a mausoleum, a monument of love, built by Shah Jahan as a final resting place of his young wife Muntaz Mahal. Started in 1631, it took twenty years to complete and it is a testament, not only of love but a magnificent example of mid 17th century skill and craftsmanship of its ancient architects and builders. Constructed in white marble and thousands of precious and semi-precious stones, all precisely inlaid, it shimmers in the bright sunlight and at sunrise and sunset glows with a warm, reddish pink hue. It is truly magnificent.

I had promised Elizabeth that she could have her photograph taken while sitting on 'that bench', where the late, Princess Diana, Princess of Wales, sat during her visit in 1992. We were in luck and Elizabeth, my Welsh Princess, was able to have the photo she had been promised. Another wish box ticked.

Elizabeth, my 'Welsh princess', at the Taj Mahal

The oppressive heat, 48.6 degrees, made it very difficult for us to wander around the rest of the site and we were very relieved to get back to the cool of our bus, totally exhausted. However, our day was far from over and a short drive took us to Agra (The Red) Fort, a huge red sandstone fort built in the Mugal style, surrounded by high walls seemingly inhabited by large numbers of monkeys. Once more we bravely ventured out into the blazing furnace of an Indian afternoon and although the fort was massively impressive, we didn't stay too long as we had another five hour drive to our next destination, Jaipur.

Our journey was a quiet one with the four of us sleeping after our early start to the day and all the walking around in the searing heat. When we finally arrived at our hotel we headed straight to the swimming pool, except for Elizabeth, who after her difficulties of the previous night, opted for a relaxing shower instead. Our friends then went out to explore the city and find somewhere to eat but we stayed in the hotel and after supper took to our beds to prepare for another full day ahead.

13
Jaipur and the Amber Fort

Today was a sightseeing tour of the 'Pink City', as Jaipur is known. A short drive took us to the truly impressive Amber Fort, a huge structure of red sandstone built cross the top of the mountains which surround Jaipur, There were three ways to get up to the fort, by foot, by vehicle or to ride on the back of an elephant. Taking pity on the old elephant and opting out of walking in the heat, we decided to be driven and once there spent the next two hours saying our 'Oh's and Ah's', at the sights of the now familiar, impressive structure of the fort and all the impressive carvings inside.

We were not being disrespectful but at that stage we were desperately more interested in finding seats in the shade away from the relentless sun.

Back in our lovely cool vehicle, which we just wouldn't have managed without and the copious amounts of bottled water we were supplied with each day, we continued our tour of the sights of Jaipur. We visited the Janta Mater (Water Palace), Hawa Laxmi (Palace of the Winds), Narayan Temple, The Old Pink City and finally the Sawat Man Singh Museum. They were all very interesting and we wished that we had more time to explore each one of them more fully and give them the time they deserved. It had been another long and tiring day and we ended the afternoon relaxing in the hotel swimming pool.

That evening we were taken back to the Amber Fort to experience a wonderful 'Sound and Light Show', which illustrated the diverse heritage and culture of North West India. Our friend Paul, had researched the best, authentic restaurants near our hotel and took us along many side streets where we had to avoid, not only the local traffic but also many animals, including several cows. The food in the restaurant was delicious and cost just a fraction of the meals in the hotel.

The next day we had another six hour drive to Delhi where we were to spend the next two nights. Another lovely hotel with yet another beautifully refreshing swimming pool to ease our tired and aching limbs before venturing out into the balmy evening to find another of Paul's eating places.

This one was in the middle of the local market and to get to it, instead of encountering traffic and cows we had to run the gauntlet of dozens of young street children, some as young as eight or nine years old, carrying small babies. It was truly heart breaking to ignore their pleas for money but we had been expressly warned not to encourage them in any way. Apparently, they were orphans and any money handed over to them would be immediately taken by them to their, 'minders', who kept out of sight in the shadows. Giving them food was a possible option but who to give it to among the many pleading hands would have been very difficult.

We felt helpless at seeing their distressed faces and guilty because we were on our way to fill our own stomachs but we understood that the only real way to help their plight was to support the many charities, Christian and others, who daily worked to help them. However, my own guilt was soon overtaken by disappointment, for having reached the restaurant I discovered that it was vegetarian!

There was little choice so I decided to order a vegetable curry and rice which to my surprise was very good indeed.

I actually really enjoyed it! Having once again to walk back past the street children who were literally outside the gates of our luxurious hotel, brought home the huge difference and the injustice in the obscene divide between the very poor and extremely rich, living in close proximity to each other. It really was distressing. We went to bed that night thanking our blessings and praying that some change will come about to address the unequal balance in the world.

14
Our Last Day

Our last full day in India and yet another full day of scheduled sightseeing. First was a visit to the beautifully serene Raj Ghat, the site of Mahatma Gandhi's cremation.

Then on to the Red Fort and Jama Masjid, the largest Mosque in India with a capacity of twenty five hundred people to worship. Followed by a bicycle rickshaw ride through the bustling local market, which was quite an experience. On to the Qutab Minar, the tallest minaret in the world (240ft,), followed by a visit to the beautiful Lotus Temple which is a Bahai House of Worship and on to Humayn Tomb. Our final visit of the day was to see the India Gate, the National War Memorial and the Tomb of the Unknown Soldier and the Eternal Flame. A lovely, sobering, place of Remembrance.

That night we went out to eat at another of Paul's recommended restaurants. Our walk took us back through the scores of the pitiful street children and although it was distressing we had, more or less, hardened our hearts to their demands but, in the circumstances there was really little we could do except resolve to support those charities that work among them. Annoyingly, despite what we had encountered, I must admit to having enjoyed our meal, during which, we talked much about our adventures with our travelling companions. They had little or no faith but were gracious enough to allow us to talk about our church life and were interested in our work in the community and for our charities. This time our adventures were part of a holiday, perhaps too long spent travelling between the 'Golden Triangle' of Agra, Jaipur and Delhi which had been a 'whistle stop' tour of beautiful and interesting sights. A tour probably designed to encourage a longer trip to both India and Nepal for some but not again for Elizabeth and probably, sadly not for me, but who knows?

Our flight home was uneventful and we were very pleased to see our Daughter, Derian, waiting for us at the airport to drive us home in her car rather than endure a long journey by bus. It really brought a happy end to our travels. Safely home, our prayers were those of thanksgiving for travelling mercies and for all those we had met and things which we had seen.

15
Reflections

As I close, bringing up to date the account of how my 'Trek of Hope', continued long after I actually finished the Trek and in fact still continues today, I am able to reflect on how, in so many ways it has changed my life.

Perhaps, following my retiring from full time work, I had been searching for something to focus on and perhaps, I may have come to a mid or late life crisis. Yes of course there was my voluntary work with the Aelwyd Housing Association, the Rainbow of Hope and of course The Leprosy Mission but in doing this valuable work of helping and serving others, it also served as a means to keep me occupied.

Yes, it could also be that I undertook the challenge of trekking in the Himalayas for my own satisfaction but having done it, I am now, more than ever, convinced that I had heard the 'Still small voice' of God, prompting me to do something in His Name and for His Glory. That I had listened and done it, despite, at some times, agreeing with those who had said, "You must be crazy!" found me receiving great blessings for my obedience to His call.

Right from the start, all the negatives for someone of my age and condition in even considering such a challenge, were staring me in the face. The obstacles, both practical and logistical, that were put in my way kept popping up, no doubt put in place by 'the other guy', only to be blown out of the way by God.

Then there were the physical and psychological struggles of actually completing each day of the climb itself. I am sure that you can guess how much of an effort it was to walk/climb for between six to eight hours each day, in thirty four degree heat and on, most afternoons, in pouring rain.

Yes it was physically tough but almost as bad, was the mental effort it took after each short stop to admire the beautiful scenery while catching my breath, to look at the seemingly endless stone steps disappearing up the steep track that lay ahead. There were times that I felt that I simply could not carry on and every time before my next move a silent prayer was uttered to spur me on.

But on I went and surprisingly (why should I be surprised?) at the end of each day I found that after just a short time and with a good meal and a refreshing cold drink inside me, I was fine. Tired limbs yes but not an ache nor a pain, nor blisters. God was certainly with me every step of the way and blessed me with a great team of Sherpas, porters and 'The Doc', as well as my wonderful, supportive and encouraging travelling companions who, through raising awareness of and funding for, their own charities, were helping others less fortunate than themselves.

As a result of my 'Trek of Hope', my various speaking engagements and magazine articles have made more people and organisations aware of the work of the two Charities, The Leprosy Mission and Rainbow of Hope that I work with and has also encouraged others to become involved in them. Through my subsequent visits to Nepal and India I have become aware of the work of 'Classrooms in the Clouds' and the plight of the Street Children in India and I am trying to help in any way I can to promote the work that is needed, not only in these countries but also in many other countries throughout the world to help those less fortunate than myself.

I write, unapologetically, from a Christian perspective while, at the same time, realising that some of you reading this book may have other faiths or no faith at all. However, I hope that everyone may be encouraged by me overcoming my struggles. While it is obviously a personal record of the challenges that lay before me, each one of us face many personal decisions every day. Generally we are able to cope with them but, occasionally, they seem insurmountable, just like a huge mountain. I simply want to share that you too can overcome your difficulties and achieve something that may seem impossible and which will enable you to overcome your own personal mountains, whatever they are and which are preventing you moving on in your life.

All that is needed is a willingness and an aim to do something, either for yourself or others, and having family and friends who will give you the much needed support for whatever it is that you are aiming to achieve. It really is that straightforward and to quote again from my dear, late, friend Paul, “Don’t just think about it, just go ahead and do it”.

I went ahead and did it and survived. While hugely difficult, it was also greatly humbling. It really was worthwhile and more rewardingly, has enabled my two Charities to benefit from the making of their work more widely known and supported through the financial gifts they received and ‘Mountains of Prayers’. Indeed, the whole of my succeeding in completing the challenge and the on-going work of the two Charities, is solidly built on the firm foundation of prayer. Not only my personal prayers but also those of countless number of family and friends whose constant prayers of support and encouragement were actually felt by me during all the difficult times I faced.

So then, let me close with a prayer. "May everyone who reads this book and all those others who have heard me speak of my struggles in facing and completing this difficult challenge, be greatly blessed and encouraged to see through and overcome their own personal 'mountains' of problems they face now or in the future." Amen.

All the many obstacles and the many thousands of steps I encountered along the way were met and conquered, yes physically by me but I was carried every step of the way, in Gods strength and for His Glory. May God bless you all.

Published by
www.publishandprint.co.uk

Printed in Great Britain
by Amazon

32290556R00096